Endorsements

This devotional is unique because it offers three different perspectives: a medical perspective, which allows you for concepts and descriptions from a health perspective. A parent's perspective, which allows you for a personal understanding of each meditation, and the perspective of a passionate student of the Word who has treasured and shaped it in his own life. For this reason and many more, I recommend that you invest time in this book.

As a Bible teacher, I always seek out a variety of references to try to illustrate and explain Scripture. In this devotional, you will find each meditation with a rich mix of different figures and definitions that will help you expand your understanding of the Word. You will receive advice from a doctor, a father and grandfather, and each reading will enrich you.

Since I was a child, I grew up seeing Saúl López from different angles: as a doctor, who always treated my entire family; as a patient father to his children (my cousins); and as a researcher and scholar of the Word of God. Now I see two more perspectives: a grandfather and a person with enough wisdom to walk through life hand in hand with the Lord, who can now look back and recommend how we live better. I personally enjoy the meditation of Psalms 42 and 91.

Luis Rene Lopez Robles
Father, husband, and Bible enthusiast;
Author of the book: *Your Children's Ministry Can Grow*;
Writer of books for children's leaders;
Pastor of Children's Church.

We appreciate Saul's authentic and biblical perspective in this book of devotions. He shares how our goal as believers is to love the Word of God and then gives practical applications on how to live in that reality. Saul's highlighted topics include walking with God, hearing from God, identity, restoration, and forgiveness, to name a few. Each devotion is complete with questions for the individual or for group discussion. This volume is an ideal manual for personal discipleship.

Steve and Marjie Schaefer
Authors and teachers
Flourish Through The Word Ministries

Endorsements

Sometimes it helps to read the Bible near someone else. Their life story connects the Word of God with your story. Your heart warms with hope.

Saul and his wife Ellen left their comfortable life in Guatemala to be close to their grandchildren in Seattle. Dr Lopez is a physician and a retired professor at a university in Central America. It's never easy to leave the comfort zone. When Saul and Ellen landed in Seattle they did not know they would step into the world-wide pandemic and lockdown in their new home.

The city was strange, the language different, the rain unending, and the friends were new.

Page by page, one day at a time, Saul lived out the promises of God. He found that there is hope. Reading the Bible together with Saul Lopez will encourage anyone who is seeking clarity in a confusing place.

If you are that person looking for hope, then this book has arrived in your hands just in time. Read it at the pace that Saul wrote these devotions, one day at a time.

Your best days are yet to come. Keep in faith!

Philip McCallum
Lead Pastor Evergreen Church, Bothell, Washington

There is HOPE

Devotions that bring comfort, strength, and peace in times of need

BY DR. SAUL LOPEZ

The English Standard Version of the Bible has Used for Scripture Unless Otherwise Noted

ISBN Ebook: 979-8-9927610-1-6
ISBN Paperback: 979-8-9927610-0-9

Artwork by Saul Lopez
Isaiah 53 Artwork by Carlos David Lopez
Published By: Saul Lopez
Interior Layout, Cover Design: Kristi Knowles

Contents

DEDICATED TO:

Ellen,
Carlos David and Fernanda,
Brett and Carey,
Joy and Matthew,
David, Luna,
Levi, Joshua, Samuel,
Andrew, Elijah, Rebecca, Hosanna

INTRODUCTION

I began writing this series of 31 devotional topics during the difficult times of the Covid-19 pandemic, with the purpose of sharing what was very helpful in a time of changes in my life: retirement from my job as a university professor during 32 years, moving to another country to be with our children and grandchildren, adjusting to a different language and culture, and then feelings of anxiety, desperation, and depression brought on by the pandemic.

The devotionals first took the form of YouTube videos. They are primarily directed to believers to strengthen their faith in God, and to non-believers, so they can come to a personal relationship with God through Jesus Christ. The topics can be used in Bible study groups, in churches, as devotionals, or for personal studies. At the end of each devotional, there are questions for meditation and group discussion.

The first devotionals are on selected Psalms and the second part on selected chapters of the book of the prophet Isaiah. Through the comfort and strength of the Word of God, we receive hope and blessing; the good news brings joy, peace and justice. All these give us encouragement, faith, strength, hope and peace. This led us to the title **THERE IS HOPE**.

Acknowledgements

To: Ellen
for the initial work in translation from Spanish, and help with the meditation and group discussion questions.

To: Carlos David
For the Illustration for Isaiah 53

To: Kristi
for her knowledgeable, patient, and personable assistance, and in helping shape the text and the rest of the process for publishing.

All He Does Prospers

Read Psalm 1

We all have both the opportunity and the privilege of building our lives, but it is best to do so with the firm and complete foundation that the sacred Scriptures give us. The Bible has counsel and all-around edification for all needs and aspects of our lives.

Psalms is a book of songs of adoration to God. The introduction contains instruction about the importance of loving and meditating on the Word of God. We all want to be happy, bear fruit (or results) and have a quality life.

In Psalm 1, each person has two options or roads or lifestyles. They can follow the psalm's instruction not to "walk in the counsel of the wicked", "nor stand in the way of sinners," "nor sit in the seat of scoffers", or instead, they can decide to do them.

It is better to do what the blessed man does, "In the law or the instruction of the Lord he delights and meditates day and night."

When we know God, the Author of this psalm, we realize His love and faithfulness in His promises, His principles, values, and plans. As a result, following His counsel will not be a burden but a delight. His counsel is a constant lifestyle. Jesus said in John 14:6, "I am the way, the truth, and the life; no man comes to the Father but by me." Psalm 119:106 says, "Your word is a lamp to my feet and a light to my path."

The Word of God is instruction that we should love, and on which we should meditate day and night. Meditation or reflection allows us to better understand what we read and to apply it to our life. 2 Timothy 3:16-17 (ESV) says, "All scripture is breathed out by God and is profitable for teaching, for reproof, for correction, and for training in righteousness, that the man of God may be complete, equipped for every good work."

As a result of drawing near to the true source of life and nutrition, we will continually bear fruit (or results) and live an abundant life. Christ said in John 10:10 (ESV), "The thief comes only to steal and kill and destroy. I came that they may have life and have it abundantly." This abundant life comes from putting our trust in God and in His Word, regardless of the heat of any circumstance, because we are near the River of Life. Doing this results in strength, bearing fruit in its time, and not being afraid before the judgment of God.

There are only two paths before us in life. We choose the one we want, but we do not get to choose the consequences of that choice; it is an inevitable result of the path we follow.

The second portion of Psalm 1 compares the person who prefers not to follow the divine counsel with the "chaff," the outside shell of the grain of wheat that is blown away with the wind. Only the wheat falls to the granary floor to be used. This person cannot stand in the congregation of the righteous.

The righteous one acknowledges his spiritual need, confesses his sins and turns away from them, and trusts in the work of Jesus Christ who took our place on the cross.

The righteous one constantly seeks the instruction of God, delights in it, reflects on it day and night to live it. He trusts in God always and sees the results in himself.

For Meditation and Group Sharing

Psalm 1 and the above devotional:

1. Who is the Author of this instruction? What do we know about Him here?

2. What kind of counsel do the ungodly or wicked give? (The ungodly are people lacking faith in God, with love for the common good, but rather they do not fear God.)

3. Nowadays, who are the scorners or ridiculers (those who ridicule in a cruel or grotesque manner) in general? They even make fun of the good and of wisdom.

4. Who in the Bible was scorned very cruelly, like none other?

5. What is the opposite of mocking?

6. Where or to whom do you go for counsel? Why?

7. Where do you find good company, associates, or partners?

8. At some time, have you had to decide not to be in constant company with people like that? How was that? What happened as the result of deciding the right way?

9. Choose a verse or phrase of Psalm 1 that will help you to be "blessed".

10. Repeat it, write it and illustrate it.

THE GREAT VALUE AND IDENTITY THAT GOD GIVES TO THE HUMAN BEING

Read Psalm 8

In this Psalm, King David begins by describing the majesty and greatness of God: in His creation, in his character, and in His works. He then describes the glory of His creation in the universe and considers how little man is. In this context he asks himself why man is so special to God, who considers him and cares for him so tenderly.

God's purpose in creating man was so he could govern over all His creation, but because of sin, man became depraved and died spiritually. Jesus humbled himself, becoming lower than the angels, to redeem man on the cross and He was glorified in His resurrection. His plan is to take many to glory as children who are born again through acceptance of the salvation of Jesus Christ, thus restoring the initial purpose of the creation of man. The human being knows his identity when he knows God and His plans.

THE GLORY OF GOD

The glory of God refers to His majesty, splendor, brightness, and His incomprehensible greatness. The name of the Lord implies His character and His Person; He is our sovereign Lord with all authority and power. His name is glorious in all the earth and over the heavens.

His glory is revealed or seen on the earth and in the heavens, but it is also seen and heard in the mouths of the little ones who praise God. When Jesus entered the temple and did miracles, children shouted: "Hosanna to the Son of David," praising Him before the indignation of religious leaders there (Matthew 21:15-16).

Children are an example to us. They come to God with sincerity, faith, and transparency, and they praise Him. God has a principle in the Bible. He uses the weak and the small to conquer His enemies, especially using praise and worship. David was the youngest among his brothers, and when he was an adolescent, he defeated the giant Goliath. Gideon was from a poor family and was the youngest of his brothers; he became a leader to free his people from their enemies.

The plan of God for man

In the beginning, God created man in His image and likeness to have dominion over His creation on earth. But due to sin, man "comes short of the glory of God" (Romans 3:23), so the Father sent His Son in the form of a human, made a little less than the angels. By dying on the cross, suffering in our place, He is the Author of Salvation of all who will believe.

> "'What is man that you are mindful of him, or the son of man, that you care for him? You made him for a little while lower than the angels, you have crowned him with glory and honor, putting everything in subjection under his feet.' Now, in putting everything in subjection to him he left nothing outside his control. At present, we do not yet see everything in subjection to him. But we see him who for a little while was made lower than the angels, namely Jesus, crowned with glory and honor because of the suffering of death, so that by grace of God he might taste death for everyone." (Hebrews 2:6-9, ESV)

He gives us identity as children of God when we receive Him as Savior and Lord.

The Christ who gives us life, perfectly represents the image and likeness of God. This image of God is being sculpted in us by the Holy Spirit: "And we all with unveiled face, beholding the glory of the Lord, are being transformed into the same image from one degree of glory to another. For this comes from the Lord who is the Spirit" (2 Corinthians 3:18, ESV).

This happens by the measure in which we allow God the Holy Spirit and His Word to renew our minds and rule our beings in His will. And we will be like Him in His coming. "Beloved, we are God´s children now and what we will be has not yet appeared; but we know that when he appears we shall be like him, because we shall see him as he is" (1 John 3:2, ESV).

God´s perfect plan is fulfilled only through Jesus Christ and in all who receive His salvation and submit to his lordship. I Corinthians 16:27 says that

God has placed all in subjection under the feet of the Lord Jesus Christ. He has been given the Name that is above all that is named in heaven, on the earth and under the earth, and every knee will bend before Him to the glory of God the Father.

God created humanity with glory, in His image and likeness, but because of sin, man was lost and he fell short of the glory of God. Only Jesus in His first coming solved the sin problem, restoring the image and likeness of God in all who have believed in His work on the cross and in His resurrection. Having acknowledged our need to be forgiven, and by believing in Jesus, we become children of God, justified by faith, and we enter into a process of restoration until His coming.

We should humble ourselves before God our Lord and acknowledge His glory and majesty, which gives us victory against our enemies. Our enemies can be fear, anxiety, and depression, among others. God saves us integrally, now and in eternity; we are special to God in whose creation we hold the highest value.

For Meditation and Group Sharing

Psalm 8 and the above devotional:

1. Name examples of "the majesty and greatness of God" in His creation, in His character, and in His works.

2. Read I Samuel 17:45-47. How did the shepherd boy David fight "with his words" against Goliath before throwing a rock.

3. What is so surprising and spectacular in "the heavens, the moon and the stars" (remember that David was looking at these without scientific instruments)?

4. How is it that the Lord "crowns man with glory and majesty?"

5. In which ways do humans "dominate" the works of the hands of the Lord?

6. Notice that David starts this psalm with "our Lord". It is one thing is to contemplate how wonderful God is; it is another thing to cry out to the Creator as "my Lord". What does this mean to you?

7. According to the devotional, how is the perfect plan of God fulfilled?

8. According to 2 Corinthians 3:18, in what process are those who have believed in the Lord Jesus and His work?

9. Write your own "psalm" or meditation to God on this topic.

How God Speaks to Us and How We Should Respond

Read Psalm 19

From his youth when he was a shepherd, David, the author of this psalm, admired nature, recognizing its greatness and beauty. He recognized the Lord, Creator of the heavens and the firmament, and he sang to the Creator with psalms. When David became king, he had the Ark of the Covenant in a tent on Mount Zion (the Ark that had been in Moses' tabernacle and later would be in Solomon's temple). In this place, David did not offer sacrifices but rather praise and worship. David was a not priest, but in this instance, the Lord allowed him to have the Ark with him as a measure of grace and favor of the God of Israel who called him "the man after the Lord's own heart" (Acts 13:22, I Samuel 13:14).

God speaks to man through nature and specifically through His Word to inspire a need to seek Him. In nature we see God's greatness, His power, intelligence, beauty, and His purpose in everything. Through His Word we know that God is interested in restoring our lives, our friendship with Him and in blessing us.

Nature:

Without words and with inaudible sounds, God has made Himself universally known to every creature. We can see the glory and majesty of God, observing the order, balance, beauty, greatness, complexity, and exactness of everything in nature. Have you stopped to look at a sunrise, a sunset, a rainbow, the birds, the animals, and to acknowledge and thank God? During any difficult situation, it is always comforting to have contact with nature and enjoy it. If we take advantage of them, the cycles of day and night bring wisdom for our benefit and for others.

We can see God's greatness, His creation, our smallness and the need we have of Him.

God with His power, beauty and love sends the heat of the sun; its warmth and light shine over all without exception. This is a representation of a just God who wants to make Himself known and save everyone.

His Word:

"The law of the Lord is perfect," or the instruction (Torah) of the Lord is perfect, complete, to restore our souls. The soul, our "I", our inner person, needs to be saved and restored. Read John 3:16 and 2 Timothy 3:15-16 (ESV). Paul says to Timothy,

> "From childhood you have been acquainted with the sacred writings, which are able to make you wise for salvation through faith in Christ Jesus. All scripture is breathed out by God and profitable for teaching, for reproof, for correction and for training in righteousness, that the man of God may be complete, equipped for every good work."

God is a God of covenants, and His testimonies are secure. Jesus said in John 6:39, "You search the Scriptures because you think that in them you have eternal life; and it is they that bear witness about me."

His Word is faithful, proven, has no errors, and feeds us. "Man shall not live by bread alone but by every word that proceeds from the mouth of God" (Matthew 4:4, Deut. 8:3). The instructions are perfect, and they cheer and heal our inner beings as we have confidence and friendship with God the author of perfect peace (Isaiah 26:3).

This peace is valuable, more precious than fine gold; it is the source of faith that saves and blesses us. It nourishes us, it is sweeter than honey that comes from the honeycomb. It is more nutritious that organic honey and pure for our whole being.

Have you stopped to read the Bible and meditate on it? If not, this is a good opportunity to make this a good habit.

Personal application:

David admonishes us to recognize our errors and known sins, and to ask

God to free us from sins that are hidden to us. One of the sins and obstacles mentioned here is pride that impedes us from receiving forgiveness, because we do not acknowledge ourselves as sinners having a need for God and His forgiveness through Jesus Christ. When we do, then we have the reward of inner peace that comes from the God who loves us and sent His Son to die for our sinful nature and our sins.

Psalm 19 ends with a decision and the desire that the meditation of his heart and the words of his mouth be pleasing, in the context of praise and worship, instead of sacrifices to God. Paul says in Romans 10:10:9-10 (ESV), "If you confess with your mouth that Jesus is Lord and believe in your heart that God raised him from the dead, you will be saved. For with the heart one believes and is justified, and with the mouth one confesses and is saved."

Have you made this decision and confession? This is a good opportunity to do it.

Finally, David professes God as his Lord, his Rock, and his Redeemer. God is the Lord of all circumstances; He is our help and security in all situations and the One who has rescued us for Him. AMEN.

For Meditation and Group Sharing

About Psalm 19 and the devotional

1. Who wrote this Psalm? How is the writer described? What is the meaning of "a man after God´s own heart" (as David was)?

2. What do you see as you observe nature? Share experiences of being in nature and experiencing comfort while in difficult situations.

3. Our current Bible has two testaments; David knew the "Torah" (the first five books of the Old Testament containing instructions and the law). Describe a few things we find in them that can "restore" or "convert the soul" (Psalms 19:8), or that "make the simple wise".

4. What should we do with the Scriptures to achieve these benefits?

5. Is it possible to read and hear the Word of God without "fear of the Lord"?

6. Do you remember a time that you experienced "delight" or "warning" from the Scriptures?

7. When we read and hear the Scriptures, we see our own sins and possible presumption or pride. What does David ask God to do with his sins?

8. What happens to the person in verses 13 and 14?

9. Write out verse 14 and include it as part of your prayer to God.

THE PRAYER OF VICTORY OVER ENEMIES

Read Psalm 20

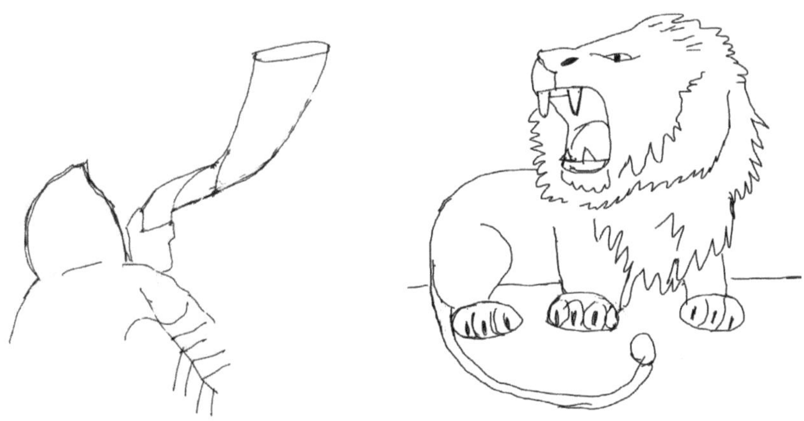

Life is full of difficulties, inside and outside of us, and we need to know how to be victorious always. 2 Chronicles 20:5-12 describes Jehoshafat, King of Judah, who had to face his enemies. They were more numerous and powerful than he, and he was afraid. Jehoshafat prayed and fasted, humbling himself and confessing his sins before the Lord God of Israel. He acknowledged the name of the Lord, the God of covenants and promises, and he made his petition. Remembering what the Lord had done in the past and in the context of his conflict, he asked for help. The Lord responded through a prophet, saying "Do not fear; the battle is not ours but God's". He guided them and gave them an adequate strategy. They believed, worshiped, and praised the Lord, and in those moments, they took the spoils of the enemies who became confused and destroyed each other.

Psalm 20 is the prayer of a king before going into battle. David was a king who had experienced battle and victories; at the same time, David is known for his example of how to praise and worship the Lord God of Israel. From his youth, he learned to know the Name of the Lord, fellowship with Him and praise Him.

In this context, we should remember that "our battles are spiritual and not against flesh and blood" (Ephesians 6:12); victory is not achieved through our efforts but by the power of the name of the Lord Jesus Christ who conquered on the cross for us.

Elements needed for victory in battle:

The name of the Lord

In this psalm, David instructs us about the elements that deliver victory in battles.

The name of the Lord, *El Adonai*, or my Lord, the eternal great I AM, our Provider, the Lord of Hosts, the God of Covenants, was known by David through his experience of fellowship and worship and in battles. This God, who is so personal, was in the "sanctuary" or "Mount Zion" in David's time. Today, He is directly with us through Jesus Christ in whom we have free entrance into the most holy place; there we have help and strength for every situation. The name of the Lord Jesus is over every name, including battles that happen (the name "Jesus" means "the Lord saves").

Offerings and sacrifices

Before battles, to solve their sin problem and to seek fellowship with God, the Israelites gave offerings and burned sacrifices. Now we know that Jesus has conquered our greatest enemies—sin, death, the evil one, the flesh and the world—on the cross and in his resurrection.

> "Who, though he was in the form of God, did not count equality with God a thing to be grasped, but emptied himself, by taking the form of a servant, being born in the likeness of men. And being found in human form, he humbled himself by becoming obedient to the point of death, even death on a cross. Therefore, God has highly exalted him and bestowed on him the name that is above every name, so that at the name of Jesus every knee should bow, in heaven and on earth and under the earth, and every tongue confess that Jesus Christ is Lord, to the glory of God the Father." (Philippians 2:6-11, ESV)

Ephesians 5:2 (ESV) says: "And walk in love, as Christ loved us and gave himself up for us, a fragrant offering and sacrifice to God." In any battle, we come to the heavenly Father in prayer in the name of the One who gave Himself for us as a perfect offering and sacrifice, giving us complete victory. The Lord provides us with the Lamb for anything we need (*Jireh* - provider); we should believe and give Him thanks.

The desires of our heart

In our hearts, with confidence, we should ask for the blessings and goodness of God in our purposes, plans, and objectives over the various aspects of our lives. Let us ask Him, according to each specific need, trusting in His Word, in His promises and in the work of Jesus Christ for us.

The option of trusting in the Lord

The Lord who saved His anointed king, has His almighty, saving right hand, Jesus (*Yeoshua* - "the Lord saves"), who is seated at the right hand of the majesty in high places. He has the name above all names. There are only two options: trust in the temporary human strength that weakens and falls, or trust in the Name of the Lord to lift us and keep us on our feet. Let us decide to trust totally in the Lord who loves us and who is faithful to His promises.

David ends saying: "O Lord, save...," Hosanna, please save us, Lord and Savior Jesus Christ, defend us, help us, respond to us, and hold us!

What is your need? We need to trust in His saving Name, believe His Word, praise Him and decide to trust in Him completely. He is your Helper, Savior, the perfect Offering and Sacrifice. The battle was already won on the cross; only in Him is there victory. He is the only one who can fulfill the desires of your heart and give you victory in every battle. Trusting in His Word, let us ask Him for what we need, and in faith, give Him thanks.

"Do not be anxious about anything, but in everything by prayer and supplication with thanksgiving let your requests be made known to God" (Philippians 4:6, ESV). AMEN.

For Meditation and Group Sharing

About Psalm 20 and the above devotional:

1. According to Psalm 20, what are all the things that David firmly believed God would do?

2. What are all the things that David and his people would do?

3. Who or what does Psalm 5 say are our worst enemies?

4. According to Philippians 2:6-11, what gave the Lord Jesus the victory to then be exalted by God?

5. According to the passage in Philippians 2, what should that inspire in us?

6. Read 2 Chronicles 20. Which other elements contributed to the victory of Jehoshaphat?

7. Twice in Psalm 20:5,7, David mentions "the name of our God." To pray like David and have faith like that, it is necessary for God to be "our God" and for us to identify fully with Him as the same Lord God as David's God. If David's God is your God, how can you have similar experiences in prayer and faith?

8. List the "elements for having victory in battles."

9. When one prays, in what should he or she trust?

The Lord is My Shepherd

Read Psalm 23

This is a classical poem that has had music throughout the centuries. It is sung praise that merits the truth of giving thanks to the Lord. David tells of his experience, given from the position of providing and caring for his sheep as a shepherd.

Through the New Testament, we know that Jesus is the Good Shepherd who gives His life for His sheep; and that Jesus Christ resurrected is the Great Shepherd to whom we have returned.

The Shepherd provides for our needs.

The Shepherd that is the Lord and God of all, is also the Provider of all. "I shall not lack anything"—starting with our deepest spiritual needs, by receiving Christ and His work on the cross by faith in our hearts.

Rest:

Our first need is to restore fellowship with the Lord. Matthew 11:28 (ESV) says, "Come to me, all you who are weary and burdened, and I will give you rest. Take my yoke upon you and learn from me, for I am gentle and humble in heart, and you will find rest for your souls." Rest is the first thing we experience in our relationship with God; He takes us to green pastures where He gives us rest. "He leads me besides still waters."

Our daily walk:

After rest comes normal daily life but now led by the Shepherd through paths of righteousness, giving honor to His name and His faithfulness. He knows the path and loves us, so it is up to us to obey through love. Along the way, there may be dark conditions that bring fear, but because the Shepherd who loves us is there, fear is cast out (I John 4:8). His rod and His staff are my strength and inspire trust. The rod is used against the enemy, and the staff is for the sheep.

Fellowship:

The Shepherd also is a Host and He sets a table (in the presence of our enemies—who may be in our minds and emotions or may be enemies outside of ourselves). At that table, there is fellowship, protection, an anointing over our heads, and our cups overflow (it is the power and great joy of God Holy Spirit in our minds). All this is result of fellowship with God.

The rest of the pilgrimage:

After being invited to fellowship with God, He sends us the goodness and mercy that we need for the rest of our pilgrimage. And at the end of the road, we will be in the house of the Father, as the children that we are, to live with Him forever.

For Meditation and Group Sharing

About Psalm 23 and the above devotional:

1. How did the writer know all these characteristics of the Good Shepherd and about the needs and care of the sheep?

2. Look for Bible passages that support the second paragraph of the devotional.

3. What do "green pastures" represent for the person that follows the Good Shepherd?

4. Sheep lie down in the pasture after eating. What can you do with the "food" from the Word of God?

5. What is the first "rest" a person has in his relationship with the Lord Jesus?

6. Research:
    - What did a shepherd do with a rod and a staff?
    - What are these compared to now in the Lord?

7. How do the "paths of righteousness" in Psalm 23 teach us how to live an upright life? What is the correlation between Psalm 23 and Psalm 1:1 in which the author decides not to do certain things?

8. What things can cause you to fear?

9. What happens with fear when you remember that the Lord is with you?

10. In Matthew 11:28-29, how does one "find rest for the soul" in the yoke of the Lord?

11. What inspiration do you find in your meditation of Psalm 23? Is it prayer, an artistic illustration, music, a poem, a message for somebody who does not know the Lord Jesus, or something else?

Restoring the Relationship with God and Worshiping

Read Psalm 24

The Lord God is the owner of the earth and all that is in it, including its inhabitants. He is worthy of recognition and worship. We are called to be good stewards of the earth and the world. Man was created in the image and likeness of God to have fellowship with Him, but due to sin, this fellowship was lost. It is important to know how to restore fellowship with the Creator to worship Him for what He is: the King of Glory.

In Psalm 24, King David gives a call to praise and worship God on his holy mountain (Mount Zion). He asks us two questions: Who will go up to the mountain of the Lord? And who will be able to stand in His holy place? Then David welcomes the Lord, the King, the Almighty Lord of Hosts, to the entrance of the city of David.

David knew the route of the Ark of the Covenant which represented the presence of God on the earth. In the time of Eli the priest, without any spiritual preparation and to be used as an amulet, the Israelites brought the Ark to a war against the Philistines, and it was captured by the enemy. The Philistines suffered many calamities while they had the Ark, and so they returned it back to Israel with offerings.

For the next 27 years, the Ark was in the house of Aminadab, and from there David took it to Jerusalem. But lacking in fear of the Lord, the Ark was carried on an ox cart, and someone touched it and died.

David then left the Ark in the house of Obed Edom for three months where it blessed him and his house.

Requirements for being in the presence of the Lord

After David calls us to praise God—who is the Owner of everything, and we are only stewards—he calls us to fellowship with God. He answers the two questions of who will go up and who will stand on the holy mountain by listing the characteristics of a righteous person.

- "He who has clean hands and a pure heart"
  Our actions and intentions must be pure.
- "He does not lift up his soul to what is false (vain things)"
  Worshipping anything that is not God—creation, and creatures or what is made by man—cannot save us and is therefore false. We must not worship, venerate, or ask for it.
- "And does not swear deceitfully"
  Honesty and all we say with our mouths is important.

These are the internal characteristics and the lifestyle of a righteous man. The result of being just is receiving the blessings and the righteousness of God of his salvation. God is just by nature and gives to each as needed. Righteousness is the perfect fulfillment of the perfect law of God. But as humans, it is impossible not to fail in something. Psalm 24 says. "There is none righteous, no, not one." This is why we need justification. Justification is the act by which God imputes or applies the righteousness of Jesus who is the only one who completely fulfilled the law and was a substitute for us on the cross.

When, by faith, we receive justification from God, we are called to abide in a righteous life, through continual repentance and faith in Jesus.

The psalm says, "Such is the generation of those who seek him, who seek the face of the God of Jacob." The Hebrew word "face" is the same as "presence" in the Bible.

"Open the doors that the King of glory may come in"

Having solved the sin problem that separates us from God, He enters Jerusalem as the King of glory. Glory, honor, and God's presence and splendor (*kabod* in Hebrew) were lost when the Ark was captured. But it was recovered, and God was seen as holy. He is now welcomed to Mount Zion, the city of David. The doors had to be opened to the King of Glory, the Strong and Mighty One, the Lord of Battles. It does not matter what kind of battle we are going through, the Lord is over all.

Before the gates were opened, David asked, "Who is this King of Glory?" The answer was "the Lord," and the gates were open. David referred to "the ancient gates" that were opened to let the King of Glory come in.

Jesus says, "Behold, I stand at the door and knock; if any man hears my voice and open the door, I will come in and eat with him and he with me" (Revelation 3:20). The victorious Jesus wants to come into our houses and hearts: the Firstborn of the Dead, He who opened the doors to the Kingdom of heaven for believers, the Lamb of God, the Lion of the Tribe of Judah, the King of Kings, Lord of Lords, with all authority in heaven and earth.

We must praise the Lord for His creation, and we have the responsibility of stewarding it. But we can only be happy in His presence when we have been justified by faith in Jesus, and when we walk in righteousness. We are part of the Eternal Kingdom!

For Meditation and Group Sharing

Psalm 24 and the above devotional

1. In this psalm, what are the characteristics and the attributes of God?

2. What does this person do, according to this psalm?

3. Read Psalm 118:10-21 and comment on the similarities with Psalm 24.

4. Read Psalm 89:5-9, 11 and compare it with this psalm.

5. Describe "pureness of hand and heart" and the "truth."

6. The "eternal (or ancient) doors" (v. 7) do not refer to eternity but to a permanent place for the Ark of God. Comment on the concept that the presence of God was wherever the Ark was.

7. Some believe that verses 9-10 may refer to the second coming of the Lord to govern. Please comment on this.

8. According to the explanation in the devotional, what is justification?

9. Write a prayer to God regarding this psalm.

Trust in the Protection of the Lord

Read Psalm 27

God the Lord is the best refuge in the worst problem. He is Light, Salvation, and Strength; if we walk with Him, He will never abandon us. His salvation, His presence and the meditation in His Word are the best refuge.

Being a young shepherd, to defend his sheep in the field, David, the author of this psalm, faced enemies like lions and bears. When he became King of Israel, he rescued the Ark of the Covenant from the Philistines and took it to the house of Obed Edom where it was for three months. At that time, God blessed Obed Edom and all he had. David then moved the Ark to Zion in Jerusalem where he spontaneously worshiped and praised the Lord without sacrifices or liturgies. At that time, when he referred to the house of the Lord, he did it in relation to the tent that housed the Ark of the Covenant, not a building.

At this time, King David was going through difficult times, and this is when he came to the Lord God as his refuge. He says, "The Lord is my light and my salvation, the strength of my life. Of whom shall I be afraid?" The word "my" is important because he appropriates God's promises.

Would you like to have an experience like David's?

MY LIGHT, MY SALVATION, MY STRENGTH:

LIGHT:

Faith in God causes us to see things better because He is Light. John 1:9 says that Jesus is the true light that gives light to everyone. In John 8:12, Jesus says: "I am the light of the world; he that follows me will not walk in darkness but will have the light of life."

SALVATION:

Jesus means "the Lord saves." John 3:16 says that Father God in His love saved us by sending His Son to die for us, so that when we believe we have eternal life. In Acts 4:12 (ESV), Peter says about Jesus, "There is salvation in no one else, for there is no other name under heaven given among men by which we must be saved."

STRENGTH:

Paul says in Ephesians 6:10, "Be strong in the Lord and in the power of his might."

PRAYER AND ACTION:

During prayer we should remember the past, like David remembered past victories that God had given him, conquering lions and bears to defend his sheep in the field. We should see the future with optimism and faith, believing and hoping, seeking the promises of God.

Our focus should be "one thing I have asked of the Lord, that will I seek after," without distractions, like Mary, Martha's sister, to whom Jesus said, "One thing is necessary and Mary has chosen the good part."

David says, "That I may dwell in the house of the Lord... to gaze upon the beauty of the Lord and to inquire in his temple." David is referring to the presence of God, as it was in the Garden of Eden with Adam and Eve before the fall. Because of the Ark with its mercy seat, David felt protected, as we are, by the blood of Christ.

DAVID OFFERED SACRIFICES OF JOY.

David called to the Lord. In Jeremiah 33:3 (ESV), God says: "Call to me and I answer you, and will tell you great and hidden things that you have not known."

David sought the face of God. 2 Chronicles 7:14 (ESV): says, "If my people who are called by my name humble themselves and pray and seek my face and turn from their wicked ways, then I will hear from heaven and will forgive their sin and heal their land."

God protects us and does not abandon us; He is even better than our fathers. If you have had a loss and have been abandoned, the Lord is there, willing to pick you up if you allow Him.

To stay strong, we need to believe in the goodness of God in any difficult situation as long as we live here on the earth.

In the recent pandemic, with all its various difficulties, the solution to all fear was, and still is, the Light, the Salvation, and the Strength of the Lord God through Jesus Christ.

Have you received the good news? I invite you to hope in the Lord and to trust in His promises.

For Meditation and Group Sharing

Psalm 27 and the above devotional

1. Verse 1: "The Lord is my light and my salvation...". Read Psalm 18:28. How do these two passages relate to each other?

2. In the Bible, which enemy army of the people of Israel "stumbled and fell" (verse 2)?

3. In verses 4-6, David associated seeking the Lord and meditating in His house with being raised above his enemies, which then resulted in his giving worship and joyful expressions. Comment on this.

4. The person who believes, seeks, and trusts in the Lord will not always escape difficulty, enemies, or false accusations. In these times there is more persecution, and there will continue to be more persecution, because of the gospel. According to verse 13, how did David manage not to grow weary?

5. Why does looking at the past and toward the future help us when we pray?

6. In order of the topics in Psalm 27, who is the Lord for you, and what do you therefore ask of Him?

7. According to the psalm, what is prevented by believing in the goodness of the Lord?

8. In which kinds of situations do you seek the face of the Lord?

9. Who are your adversaries? What do you ask of the Lord regarding them?

10. Do you believe in the goodness of the Lord? How do you tell Him?

Blessings and Liberation that Forgiveness Brings

Read Psalm 32

What makes us happy? Something external? Circumstances, money, the approval of others? There is a happiness that comes from the forgiveness of God. The name "Judah" in Hebrew means "recognition" and at the same time "praise and thanksgiving."

With so many problems, we can still be part of the solution when we do a self-evaluation to identify problems and solve them. The greatest and most important problem of humanity is not our circumstances or other people, but the sin which separates us from God. This has been the same problem from the beginning. "The wages of sin is death, but the gift of God is eternal life in Christ Jesus our Lord" (Romans 6:23). This death is the separation from God and with that comes destruction, but in this, "God showed his love, in that while we were yet sinners, Christ died for us" (Romans 5:8), so that through the elimination of guilt for sin He would give pardon, spiritual life, and peace.

The inner peace that the Lord gives us is overall peace: with Him, with ourselves and with others. It is not dependent on external circumstances, because it is internal and relies on our relationship with God. This relationship or fellowship with God brings complete peace, liberation, happiness, and praise. This becomes reality when we accept by faith the work of Christ on the cross; we recognize our sins, confess them and turn from sin and draw near God.

The indicator or signal that we have been forgiven by God is inner peace, joy, and happiness that are manifested externally and impact our surroundings. In Psalms 32, King David instructs us about the great blessings that forgiveness brings, the liberation from the guilt of sin, the care we should take to not live a double life, as well as the protection and direction that God gives us.

The blessing of forgiveness

King David is instructing us about the great blessing and happiness one experiences upon receiving forgiveness of sins from the Lord. God is just, and according to Exodus 34:6-7 (ESV),

> "Then the Lord, the Lord, a God merciful and gracious, slow to anger, and abounding in steadfast love and faithfulness, keeping steadfast love for thousands, forgiving iniquity and transgression and sin, but who will by no means clear the guilty, visiting the iniquity of the fathers on the children and the children's children, to the third and the fourth generation."

The Lord is merciful and forgives the sinner but is just and gives to each according to their need, even with generational consequences. Hebrews 9:13-14 (ESV) says,

> "If the blood of goats and bulls, and the sprinkling of defiled persons with the ashes of a heifer, sanctify for the purification of the flesh, how much more will the blood of Christ, who through the eternal Spirit offered himself without blemish to God, purify our conscience from dead works to serve the living God?"

The blood of Christ his Son cleanses us from all sin when we confess it before God.

"The wages of sin is death," and that is what Jesus came to do in His first coming: to atone (eliminate the guilt for sin), to acquit, or leave without guilt the sinner who repents, and thus be merciful (sacrifice that satisfies the divine justice) to restore the sinner to fellowship with God.

Transgression (rebellion against the law of God) is forgiven, sin (missing the target, committing evil acts) is covered, canceled, and cleansed, and iniquity (life contrary and in rebellion against God) is imputed or placed on the Lamb of God that takes away the sin of the world.

But for forgiveness to occur in man (*Adam*—mankind), there must be a recognition of the need for a Savior, and a sincere acknowledgement of sin without excuses. Confession of sin is part of that acknowledgement and includes repentance (turning away from sin and changing of the mind). This is why Proverbs 28:13 says, "Whoever conceals his transgressions will not prosper, but he who confesses and forsakes them will obtain mercy." The result of revealing and confessing our sins before God is prosperity and His mercy.

I John 1:9 says, "If we confess our sins, He is faithful and just to forgive us our sins and to cleanse us from all unrighteousness." Forgiveness and inner cleansing come. If we do not cover up our sin before God but confess, we obtain holiness in our souls, emotions, minds and even in our bodies.

LIFESTYLE:

A life of fellowship with God is a restoration that requires constant confession of known sins in order to draw nearer to God and to be more victorious. Psalm 32: 6 (ESV) says, "Therefore let everyone who is godly offer prayer to you at a time when you may be found, surely in the rush of great waters, they shall not reach him." This restoration includes not only confession of sin, but casting off emotional burdens, and asking and receiving help in times of need.

The Lord is a safe refuge for those who have fellowship with Him, even though He will be the Judge for those who reject him today, because He is just. He is a refuge. He guides us and teaches us in the right way through His Word and His Spirit when we have fellowship with Him.

The counsel of a person who has been forgiven is to obey in love and respect for God. This is for our good and keeps us from being like a horse or a mule that requires a bit, bridle and reins in order to turn around, by using strength and with pain. For our good and prosperity, it is better to learn by following this advice instead of learning from pain. According to the law of sowing and reaping, if someone chooses the way of sin, he will harvest great pain; but if we choose fellowship with God, His mercy and blessings will follow us. When we receive the plan of God that He provides in His justice and love on the cross, we should come to Him in sincerity, confessing our faults and sins, turning from them and changing our attitudes. This brings the fruit of peace, happiness, and fellowship with God.

When we do a constant self-evaluation, we should be specific in naming the sins we need to conquer, confess them before God without excuse, believe and accept that Jesus died for all our sins and that God is faithful and just to forgive us and to cleanse us from all unrighteousness. The fruit and result of this will be peace, happiness, and joy. "Be glad in the Lord, and rejoice, O righteous, and shout for joy, all you upright in heart!" (v. 11). We are not perfect, but we are sincere and have the desire to be free in our souls and in our whole beings.

For Meditation and Group Sharing

Psalm 32 and the above devotional

1. Why is an unforgiven person not happy or content?

2. According to the psalm, what does our peace depend on?

3. Research and describe these important terms of the faith:
    - Atonement:
    - Acquit:
    - Propitiation:
    - Forgiveness:
    - Confession:
    - Repentance:

4. Research the importance of:
    - knowing God through being constantly in His Word, the Bible.
    - fellowship with the Holy Spirit.

5. Comment on verse 10.

6. What does verse 11 have to do with the rest of the chapter?

7. There is a common thought in the beginning and ending of this chapter. What is it?

8. We have an invitation (an urgency) to open our hearts and bring before the Lord all that is unconfessed and that has brought heaviness, pain, and anguish. He gives pardon, freedom, and joy. What is your response to this invitation?

PRAISING THE LORD IN DIFFICULT TIMES

Read Psalms 34

This psalm of David is a song and instructs on the need to praise the Lord God in every circumstance. When we seek, cry out and trust in the Lord, He sets us free from fear and anguish, He defends us and supplies our every need; He is our Redeemer. We must seek Him, cry out, and trust in Him; guard our thoughts, words, and actions with reverential respect toward the Lord.

Before becoming king of Israel, David, being a warrior-praiser, went through a series of difficulties and persecution by the enemies of Israel. He fled to the land of the Philistines, where King Achish received him. But the Philistine servants were suspicious of him, because David was an Israelite. David pretended to be crazy to be banished by them. When he returned to Israel, David took refuge in the cave of Adullam where several needy men joined him and were part of his army.

This is the setting for David's advice and instruction in the song of Psalm 34.

Praise, seek, cry out, humble self, and fear the Lord

His first counsel is to praise the Lord always and in any circumstance. Paul and Silas were freed after they sang hymns to God while imprisoned (Acts 16:25).

To seek the Lord (*Adonai, Hashem*) is a decision. God is the God of covenants, the same yesterday, today and forever. He is faithful, He loves us and promises to respond.

"My soul makes its boast in the Lord."

"Oh, magnify the Lord with me," He inhabits the praises of his people. There is always victory in His presence. Would you like to praise Him now?

"I sought the Lord, and he answered me and delivered me from all my fears." (Jesus said, "ask", "seek", and "knock".) He frees us from all fear: of loneliness, of the future, of abandonment and any others. Only Christ is the solution. He says: "Come to me, all you that are weary and heavy laden, and I will give you rest..." (Matthew 11:28). "Let us then with confidence draw near to the throne of grace, that we may receive mercy and find grace to help in time of need" (Hebrews 4:16, ESV). He responds and saves us. Salvation is liberation and is for our whole being: spirit, soul, and body.

Those that looked to Him were illuminated or radiant. There is grace and peace from God the Father and the Lord Jesus Christ (see Numbers 6:24). He is seated at the right hand of the majesty of God, interceding for us as High Priest.

"This poor man cried, and the Lord heard him and saved him out of all his troubles."

- Have you cried out to the Lord with an attitude of need and humility?

"The angel of the Lord encamps around those who fear him and delivers them."

- To fear the Lord is to have reverent respect for Him, it is being conscious of His presence to thank Him in thoughts, words, and actions; it is to administer our time, talents and gifts.

"Taste and see."

- We do not question the taste of honey, but its sweetness and quality are an experience.

"The young lions suffer want and hunger, but those who seek the Lord lack no good thing." (v. 10, ESV).

- See Matthew 6:33.

"Come, o children, listen to me, I will teach you the fear of the Lord."

- He does not refer to playing the harp or how to use the sword.

Life with quality and abundance comes from the fear of the Lord, keeping our tongues from evil and deceit, seeking and following peace.

If you are going through any difficulty, talk to the Lord, knowing that He is faithful and He loves you. We are justified before God only by faith and we have peace with Him through the Lord Jesus Christ. The Lord listens to any who call to Him and seek Him with an attitude of humility. Respect and fear of the Lord brings life and keeps us and frees us from all afflictions. He rescues us from sin, by His blood with which He made a covenant with whoever will believe and receive Him. "There is no condemnation for those who are in Christ" and take refuge in Him.

If you have lost a loved one, if you are frustrated, anxious, depressed or feel that you are in the cave like David was, Jesus says: "Come to me all you that weary and heavy laden, and I will give you rest." He frees the one who has been justified and seeks a righteous life. Receive the Lord as your Refuge, your Liberator; He is your Doctor and your Lawyer. Give Him thanks and praise Him.

For Meditation and Group Sharing

Psalm 34 and the above devotional

1. Where was David when he was inspired by these thoughts?

2. Who is the main character in the psalm?

3. In a few words, complete what David says (ESV):
   - Verses 1-3 instructs us to ____________________
   - Verses 4-7 say ____________________
   - Verses 8-11 call children to ____________________
   - Verses 12-18 calls to certain actions: ____________________ ____________________
   - Verses 19-22 affirms ____________________ ____________________

4. Recall experiences in which you were afraid and cried out to the Lord.

5. Look for the word "all" in the chapter and make observations.

6. What is "the fear of the Lord"? (We saw this in a previous psalm in this series).

7. Write out one or two verses of this psalm to memorize.

How to Get Out of the Pit of Despair

Read Psalm 40

David went through great difficulties that created emotional burdens of anxiety, stress, uncertainty, and despair. David felt like he was in a deep well or pit in darkness, standing in mud. All he could do was look upward to the Lord and cry out for help.

During times of diverse difficulties, such as the situation caused by the pandemic, one can despair and lose hope, and an uncertainty of the future can arise due to job loss, loss of possessions, financial problems, health problems, and others.

How to get out of the pit of despair

In his song, David first instructs that we should cry out to the Lord; anything besides Him is false or limited, because only God has a genuine interest and the ability to help us. Then, David waits on the Lord, patiently.

To cry out is to shout asking for help, with a prayer that comes from the innermost being.

Hope is the confident and certain expectation of something in the future.

Patience is perseverance, abiding, steadfastness. Impatience brings stress, frustration, and anger.

Jeremiah 33:3 (ESV) says: "Call to me, and I will answer you and tell you great and hidden things that you have not known." God knows our needs, but when we cry out and hope, He teaches us during the process, and He responds to us. He leans down to listen to us always and gets us out of the pit, puts us on the rock, and sets our steps firmly. Waiting with perseverance is important to permit God's benefits to work in us.

This is called salvation: The rock is Christ who is our Savior and our Path. There is solidness and security in Christ. Even though the future may seem uncertain, if we follow Him, He knows the best way. He is "the way, the truth, and the life; no man comes to the Father but by" Him.

Salvation always brings happiness, joy, and a new song. Israel was able to sing a new song when it was set free in the desert outside of Egypt. When one experiences salvation, others will benefit when they see this, and they will also fear and trust in the Lord.

In this moment we realize the innumerable wonders that the Lord has done, what He did in our great salvation and what He has done as we look into the past and observe those who are around us and what is around us.

The blood sacrifices, offerings and burned offerings, have ceased according to Hebrews 10:5-7, 10 (ESV):

> "Sacrifices and offerings you have not desired, but a body have you prepared for me; in burnt offerings and sin offerings you have taken no pleasure. Then I said, Behold, I have come to do your will, O God... By that will we have been sanctified through the offering of the body of Jesus Christ once for all."

Matthew 17:5 says: "A voice from heaven said: This is my beloved Son in who I am well pleased; hear him." He is a Sacrifice sufficient for our justification, to live a righteous life and to be accepted in the presence of God.

As we hear the Word of God, by faith, we open our spiritual ears, and we obey His Word in love.

The proclamation of the gospel of good news includes justification by faith and a righteous life, because God is just, merciful, and faithful. "The wages of sin is death, but the gift of God is eternal life in Christ Jesus our Lord" (Romans 6:23).

He saves us from our enemies, internal enemies, our innumerable ills, and our iniquities. He saves us and helps us when we come in the name of Jesus, confess our sins, and turn from them; from external enemies around us and mockers. The Lord defends us and saves us.

We should seek the Lord in prayer and study and meditate on His Word. Joy and happiness will come from this. Let us "say continually: Great is the Lord!". This also brings love for His salvation, for Jesus Christ.

In Summary

When we have any need, we should pray from our inner being, knowing that God the Lord knows us individually. He is our help and our Savior-Liberator, who helps us promptly if we believe and cry out. He puts us on a rock and sets our steps; He gives us hope and salvation.

For Meditation and Group Sharing

Psalm 40 and the above devotional

1. List some examples of people who are “proud” or “those who go astray after a lie" (or falsehood - see verse 4).

2. Comment on the phrase “None can compare with you”.

3. Read Hebrews 7:25-28; Hebrews 8:6-7, Hebrews 9:11-12, 15, 23-25, 28 and Hebrews 10:10-18. Explain why Jesus was “an offering and sacrifice enough for our justification.”

4. In verses 9-10, after being rescued from his despair, David presents an important response. Comment.

5. According to verse 11, what moves the Lord to act on behalf of people who are weak, fallen, and desperate?

6. Verses 12-15 speak about David's enemies that overtook him. Who or what were they?

7. Respond in your own words: In my affliction and need, My God, you are ...

Treatment for Depression

Read Psalm 42

Depression is a feeling of being lost, empty, sad, nostalgic, with painful memories and related difficulties. It is a deep feeling in the soul. The soul is made up of feelings, intellect, and the will. Depression is a feeling and a deep need that can be filled only with the presence of God.

The feeling of being lost may come from being far from the presence of God, like we see in Psalm 42. The author of this psalm was in exile far from Jerusalem and the Ark of the Covenant; he was in a faraway place in the desert, amid a pagan people, desiring to serve God in Jerusalem.

The state of depression can also come from the loss of loved ones, things, or work, or from being far from family, and also other losses, such as have come in the recent pandemic. Other than organic causes—such as hormones, thyroid disease and other illnesses—depression is a feeling and a deep problem that can only be relieved and solved by God and His presence.

Thirst

The need for water is vital; we cannot be without water for more than three days. Deer are an interesting example: a deer runs and pants, tired from seeking water to quench intense thirst. When it finds streams of water, it submerges its head and drinks until it is satisfied.

John 7:37-38 (ESV) says, "On the last day of the feast, the great day, Jesus stood up and cried out, 'If anyone thirsts, let him come to me and drink. Whoever believes in me, as the Scripture has said, 'Out of his heart will flow rivers of living water'".

Isaiah 55:1 (ESV) says, "Come, everyone who thirsts, come to the waters, and he who has no money, come, buy and eat..." Thirst is a condition that needs to be satisfied; the thirst in the soul is an inner desire that cannot be filled with anything or anybody, only with the Spirit of God and with His Word.

Depression:

Depression is fed with sadness and by hearing negative words (they said to the psalmist: "Where is your God?").

It remembers negative past events; things from the past should instead teach us.

The solution:

A person who is depressed first needs to do a self-examination. "Why are you cast down, O my soul...?"

At the same time, he needs to talk to his soul—speak to himself, the spirit speaking to the soul. "Why are you cast down, O my soul, and why are you in turmoil within me? Hope in God; for I shall again praise him, my salvation and my God."

We must speak to our souls in faith and hope, and praise God. We should express our feelings, especially in prayer to God and describe our feelings just as they are: "Deep calls to deep at the roar of your waterfalls..." In faith, we should also recognize that there is a greater power. "By day the Lord commands his steadfast love, and at night his song is with me, a prayer to the God of my life." Even if it seems contradictory, we should express our feelings as they are, and at the same time, in faith, proclaim God's mercy, praise Him and profess Him as "the Rock", our Salvation and Hope. We pray in faith, with hope and praise.

Then once again, we speak to our soul. "Why are you cast down, O my soul. Hope in *Elohim*! I must praise Him. He is the salvation of my being, and He is my God."

We must recognize that the deepest needs of our inner being are satisfied only by God, His Spirit, and His Word. We should feel the inner need, seek the Living Water, believe, drink and be satisfied.

"Is anyone among you suffering? Let him pray" (James 5:13, ESV). In this prayer, one must voluntarily do a self-examination, express what is inside, confess Jesus Christ as Lord and Savior, believe in His work and drink from the water of eternal life.

He who drinks of passing water will thirst again, but he that drinks of the water of Christ will have eternal life.

> "Jesus said to her, everyone who drinks of this water will be thirsty again, but whoever drinks of the water that I will give him will never be thirsty again. The water that I will give him will become in him a spring of water welling up to eternal life" John 4:13-14 (ESV).

AMEN.

For Meditation and Group Sharing

Psalm 42 and the above devotional

1. Describe an occasion when you were "thirsty" for something. Maybe you knew or did not know that it was your need of God.

2. It is common in difficult situations to ask the same question. Why? But the answer to "why" is not the solution. The solution is in ____.

3. Comment on the differences in what the psalmist remembers in verses 4 and 5.

4. The psalmist sometimes speaks to _____ (whom?) and at other times to ____.

5. From the devotional, what can "temporary water" represent?

6. The psalmist expresses a repeated struggle between the voices that shout to him and what he knows from God. Describe this struggle.

7. What treasure do you find in these other texts about "waiting on the Lord":
   - Isaiah 40:31
   - Psalm 130:5,7
   - Lamentations 3:22-26
   - Others

Prayer of Moses for Wisdom and Grace

Read Psalm 90

Moses, the leader and writer of the first five books of the Bible who spoke with God face to face, instructs us in this song prayer. He probably wrote this psalm for the new generation that was about to enter the promised land. In Exodus, there is also a psalm of Moses about the Israelites' exit from Egypt. There is another psalm of Moses in Deuteronomy about the time before they entered Canaan (in addition to Psalm 90), and another one is in the book of Revelation.

Moses had seen several generations; he had seen the ungodliness of Egypt, the plagues, the rebellion of Israel in the desert, the death of many, and the death of his siblings. For water to come out, he struck the rock with anger instead of speaking to it, and this was the reason he was not allowed to enter Canaan. Even so, God was, and has been, and will be, the refuge for those who seek Him and find Him, receive His mercy and salvation, and obey Him in love.

Refuge in God:

A refuge is a place that provides safety and shelter against inclement weather, danger, and enemies. The eternal God is more than a refuge for those who come to Him in times of need. Deuteronomy 33:27, (ESV) says, "The eternal God is your dwelling place, and underneath are the everlasting arms." (This verse is the last part of Moses' blessings for Israel before he died.) A refuge is a place of rest, of happiness and of fellowship with God through Jesus Christ who is the way to God the Father.

Sin has consequences that have affected mankind ("The wages of sin is death...," Romans 6:23a). Our sins are exposed before God, but even so, He loves us. Romans 6:23b: "...But the gift of God is eternal life through

Jesus Christ our Lord." I Timothy 2:5-6 (ESV) says, "There is one God, and there is one mediator between God and men, the man Christ Jesus, who gave himself as a ransom for all, which is the testimony given at the proper time." We must acknowledge our sins, confess them, repent, and receive by faith the good news of Christ dying on the cross for us. God has authority to judge mankind and His people; He knows us and calls us to believe and take refuge in Him.

THE BREVITY OF LIFE:

Human life is short, and we should use our time wisely. For the eternal God, a thousand years are as a day. We should depend on Him, seek and ask for wisdom to live, and learn to count our days, not only count things or money. As Moses says: "Return, O Lord! How long? Have pity..."

"The years of our life are seventy, or even by reason of strength eighty; yet their span is but toil and trouble; they are soon gone, and we fly away" (verse 10). Even though Moses lived 120 years, he knew that the average life span was short. "Teach us to number our days that we may get a heart of wisdom." His request is to learn to count and evaluate the days daily until wisdom comes to our inner beings. Wisdom is the correct application of what we know; its beginning is the fear of the Lord. Wisdom is being conscious that we are always before Him, and we must correctly steward what we have.

True satisfaction comes through His mercy, His grace, and His peace, through Jesus Christ. We need wisdom to not waste the time we have, to have a useful life, seeking to please God and serve our neighbor. Ephesians 5:16 says that we should take advantage of time because days are evil.

To have a fruitful life, we should ask God what His purpose is for us, so that our work is not in vain, and that we live a life of satisfaction and success.

IN SUMMARY:

- We need to recognize God as a refuge and we need His wisdom to live, because life is short.
- God is just; our sins are exposed before Him, so we need His mercy and forgiveness through Jesus Christ.
- We need to pray for wisdom to understand the brevity of life and to find our refuge in God.
- We should take advantage of time instead of being anxious or burdened with our work.
- We need to please God and to serve our neighbor.
- We should be productive and live to prepare for eternity; life is fragile and temporary.

For Meditation and Group Sharing

Psalm 90 and the above devotional

1. Another term for "refuge" could be "dwelling place". Identify the differences between the two?

2. In verse 7, where had Moses seen the wrath of God?

3. Considering the brevity of life, what does the psalmist need and ask for?

4. As you consider the brevity of life, what do you need and what would you ask for?

5. According to verses 14 and 17, what would satisfy and bring joy to the psalmist?

6. Even though the author has seen affliction, trouble and the wrath of God (vs. 7, 9), what does he declare about God?

7. The subtitle for Psalm 90 is "A Prayer of Moses, the man of God". After reading this psalm, why do you think Moses is called "man of God"?

8. Some of us have gone through struggles and thoughts like the psalmist´s. If you wrote a psalm, what might its subtitle be "Prayer of ___, man or woman __________"?

9. What is your "prayer for wisdom and grace"?

How to Have Protection and Security in Difficult Times

Read Psalm 91

In any situation we face in life, our confidence and security do not depend on what is temporary, but on God who is eternal. God is a refuge, the owner of time, and has control of everything. He is our Creator and our Redeemer through the work of his Son Jesus Christ. The good news is that salvation ensures our security and protects us from visible and invisible enemies, both internal and external.

Psalm 91 is a poem that describes a warrior, King David, who is in battle. In his language of war, he uses the terms castle, buckler, shelter, arrows, pestilence, and at the end, instead of simply surviving, he is victorious! His victory comes from totally trusting in the God of Israel. His secret was knowing God personally as the Most High, the Almighty and as his Lord. David put his trust and his love in his Lord, who freed him from his enemies and showed His salvation.

Conditions for having God's protection:

We must dwell in the shelter of the Most High and abide under the shadow of the Almighty. To dwell is to reside and be in God's presence as part of His family. We achieve this through Jesus Christ. Jesus said, "I am the way, the truth and the life; no man comes to the Father but my me." The Apostle Peter said, "There is salvation in no one else, for there is no other name under heaven given among men by which we must be saved" (Acts 4:12, ESV). Fellowship with God is through Jesus Christ, reading and studying His Word and talking to Him spontaneously in prayer.

We should know His Name; the triune God reveals Himself through His names which manifest His character and who He is and what He does for us.

- The Most High (*'El Elyon*) refers to God as the greatest of all who has control of everything, who loves us and is faithful to His promises.
- The Almighty (*'El Shaddai*) is the omnipotent God who guides us in paths of righteousness; when we follow His shadow, we see and experience His powerful works.
- My Lord (*'El Adonai*): when we submit to His lordship and obey, He keeps us and defends us.

Our relationship with God

"I will say to the Lord: My refuge and my fortress, my God, in whom I trust." This is a verbal confession, the result of a heart of faith. Romans 10:9 says: "If you confess with your mouth that Jesus is Lord and believe in your heart that God raised him from the dead, you will be saved." This implies we make God our refuge in any difficulty, giving Him our love, obeying His Word and knowing His names which benefit us directly. He is Savior (Jesus), Most High, Almighty, and He is my Lord. We should always cry out whenever we have any need.

His promises:

The Lord will free us from the snare of the fowler (trap of the hunter), from deadly pestilence, and with His wings He covers us. His faithfulness and truth are our protection. He will always give us victory over temptation. He frees us from fear. "You will not fear the terror of the night nor the arrow that flies by day... No plague will come near your tent." God promises to send angels that protect you in all your ways... "You will tread on the lion and the adder, the young lion and the serpent (dragon, spiritual being) you will trample underfoot."

Lastly, he reminds us of the importance of holding fast to God. "Because he holds steadfast to me in love..." "When he calls to me, I will answer him, I will be with him in trouble. I will rescue him and honor him. And show (make to see) him my salvation (or to enjoy salvation)."

IN SUMMARY:

Take this opportunity to reflect and do a self-evaluation.

- Evaluate our relationship with God and His salvation through faith in Jesus Christ.
- What do we have to acknowledge, confess, and leave behind, to draw near and dwell in the shelter of the Most High and under the shadow of the Almighty?
- We should put in Him our trust and our love and enjoy our great salvation.

For Meditation and Group Sharing

Psalm 91 and the above devotional

1. What does the soul need after receiving Jesus as Savior and Lord?

2. Research ancient castles and fortresses. Many from history still exist. What does the psalmist say about them?

3. This psalm mentions security and protection from various evils, but there are no promises that they will not come. When we endure hardship, according to the psalmist, what should we do?

4. How does this promise of God inspire you: "I will be with him (or her) in anguish"?

5. What is the last word of the psalm (ESV)? What name in the Bible means or refers to this word?

6. Who 'put his foot" on "the serpent" (verse 13)?

7. According to the psalm, who benefits from these promises of the Lord?

8. How do you seek to be the person "who abides in the secret place of the Most High" or "dwell under the shadow of the Almighty"?

"It is Good to Give Thanks to the Lord"

Read Psalm 92

Giving thanks to God in everything and for everything is good, because He is worthy and because He gives us internal freedom and emotional and physical health. We should give thanks to the Lord because is Creator and Giver of all good. He is Redeemer and He justifies by faith in Jesus Christ.

We should thank God for His presence, His provision, restoration, His plans and purpose for us and His eternal kingdom. Praise and gratitude to the Lord should be in peace, in rest and by singing, giving thanks to *Adonai* (my Lord), to *Elyon* (the Most High), for His works. He is "on high" whether we believe this or not. The righteous have benefits: they are strong like the buffalo, majestic like the palm and cedar trees, and they testify of the righteousness of God.

Psalm 92 was a song for the day of rest when there was only one activity, praising God. In Christ, we now have rest and victory amid any situation. It is good to praise (give thanks) to the Lord because He is worthy, because it is healthy for our whole being, because God is good, and for all the good we receive from Him. It is good to sing psalms to the Most High God who is over all. Acts 17:28 (ESV) says, "for in him we live and move and have our being" and we depend on Him.

How to live what we sing:

First, the instruction is to "declare ("publish") your steadfast love [mercy] in the morning". Mercy is the willingness to have compassion on others who are suffering, especially to forgive. The passage also says "your faithfulness by night". The Lord is a God of covenants, and He is faithful. His love and faithfulness are reasons to always give Him thanks, morning and night.

From the moment we first wake up (in Hebrew: *baboker*, first hour when we wake up) and until night, gratitude continues to free us from anxiety and worry and gives us rest and peace. An appropriate atmosphere for praise, based on the Scripture, is "with music and instruments" which brings us healing and freedom.

"For you, oh Lord, have made me glad by your work; at the works of your hands, I sing for joy." We should remember and acknowledge the works of the Lord and His creation; He made man in his image and likeness. He rescues us personally through Jesus Christ His Son. John 6:29 says, "This is the work of God, that you believe in him who he has sent." We should praise Him and acknowledge Him in our lives, believing and following eternal principles.

The second instruction is to live a righteous life. There are only two options to live before God: to be righteous or foolish.

The righteous man is justified by faith and is justified by God and His grace, to live a righteous life according to the principles and values of His Word.

The foolish man acts without principles or fear of God and does not accept His existence. But even so, God's principles are eternal. "He that believes in the Son of God has eternal life; he that does not believe will be condemned" (John 3:17). Even though the fool may flourish for a time, his end is destruction, and with his eyes and ears, the righteous witness his destruction.

Our enemies are spiritual (Ephesians 6:10) and we must strengthen ourselves in the Lord and in the power of His might. Christ has conquered death on the cross and in His resurrection; He is alive now. "But you, O Lord, are on high forever."

The benefits of the righteous:

Here, King David personalizes these benefits:

"You have exalted my horn like that of the wild ox [buffalo]."

- The buffalo is a symbol of power; it is fast and very strong amid difficulties.

"You have poured over me fresh oil."

- David was anointed with oil to become king of Israel. I Samuel 16:13: "Samuel took the horn of oil and anointed him in the midst of his brothers. And the Spirit of the Lord rushed upon David from that day forward." (ESV).

- Oil is a symbol of the Holy Spirit. Acts 1:8 says: You will receive power when the Holy Spirit comes upon you, and you will be my witnesses..."

"As the palm tree will flourish and grow like the cedar in Lebanon":

- A palm tree is very tall—up to almost 100 feet. It can live more than 100 years, and its leaves are always green. At 60 to 80 years of age, the date palm can produce over 220 pounds of dates a year. Palms live in the desert and adapt to the climate, but they have deep roots—over 18 feet down with a radius of almost 60 feet.

- The cedar of Lebanon is strong and of good quality, but it grows slowly. The cedar is the national tree of Lebanon and is the symbol of happiness and prosperity; it is characterized by its density and durability. Solomon used these in the construction of the temple.

The righteous are "planted in the house of the Lord"

- They will flourish in the courts, a place where offerings are made for sin.
- "They still bear fruit in old age; they are ever full of sap and green". This promise is bearing fruit, vigor and an abundant life with purpose, a productive life to the end. Instead of experiencing anxiety or depression, the righteous will be firm, robust, and healthy, watered and fertilized by the word of God. Their purpose is "to declare that the Lord is upright; he is my rock, and there is no unrighteousness in him."

IN SUMMARY:

God, the Most High, is righteous. He loves us, and if we receive the salvation of Jesus Christ, He justifies us by faith. He gives us strength through His Holy Spirit who enables us to bear fruit in the midst of any difficult situation. Even in old age, we are tasked with bearing fruit, and being a blessing, and being blessed. Because of this, the Lord is worthy of all praise and of continually giving Him thanks. AMEN

For Meditation and Group Sharing

Psalm 92 and the above devotional

1. According to the devotional, how does giving thanks provide internal deliverance and emotional and physical health?

2. In verses 7 and 9, which actions apply to the evil ones?

3. Throughout the Bible, the words "but God" or "but you, God" identify a contrast. Look for examples of this.

4. Verse 10 says, "I have been anointed with fresh oil." Read Psalm 45:7 and identify the similarities in these two passages.

5. In the psalm there are verbs associated with planting: planted, sprout, grow, bloom, bear fruit. How do these words apply to our life in the Lord?

6. The psalmist recommends "announcing in the morning your goodness and your faithfulness in the evening". Why do you believe these recommendations are shown in this order?

7. What can you do to "announce" in the morning and in the evening?

Reasons to Bless the Lord

Read Psalm 103

In his old age, the author of this psalm, the valiant warrior and singer of Israel, counsels us on how to manage our souls. The soul is our inner person, the person composed of our thoughts, emotions and will. When we come to Christ and are saved—receiving Him as Savior and Lord—our souls need to be recalibrated. They need to be led by the Word of God instead of by negative circumstances, thoughts or emotions.

Who is the Lord? What has He done for us?

David says, "Bless the Lord, O my soul, and all that is within me, bless his holy name!... And forget not all his benefits..." He is speaking in first person singular, and he is motivating himself to see the character of the Lord and what He has done, to bless Him with words and praise.

First, he tells himself to bless the name of the Lord. Then he mentions five benefits that come from this. The first is the forgiveness of all my iniquities, and the second, the healing of all my sicknesses.

In Isaiah 53:4 we see the Lamb of God, the Messiah who was bruised for our sins, the punishment for our peace was on Him, and by his stripes we have been healed. Exodus 15:26 says: "If you will diligently listen to the voice of the Lord your God, and do that which is right..., I will put none of the diseases on you that I put on the Egyptians, for I am the Lord, your healer." We must listen to these words with faith, believe them, and confess them with our mouths.

Another benefit is that He rescues my life from the pit. He bought me with the precious blood of Christ and that ransom, or redemption, will be completed on the day of resurrection.

Other benefits are here in our earthly race. He crowns you with steadfast love and mercy, satisfies you [your years] with good, renewing your strength and vision like what happens with the eagle, to fulfill your objectives and goals in life.

The character of the Lord is worthy of praise.

The Lord is just, and He gave His commandments for the good of His people. In the covenant through His Son, Jesus Christ, He has shown very sublime mercy. "For as high as the heavens are above the earth, so great is his steadfast love toward those who fear him." "By grace are you saved through faith, and that not of yourselves, lest anyone boast" (Ephesians 2:8).

He forgets our sins when we confess them and turn away from them; "as far as the east is from the west, so far does he remove our transgressions from us". He also shows compassion to those who fear him "as a father shows compassion to his children." He knows our vulnerable condition: Man withers like the grass and the flower, in contrast to the eternity of the Lord and His mercy.

He has established His kingdom, and we are in an era to soon see the coming of the King and Lord. The psalmist's invitation to bless the Lord is given to "his angels, mighty ones who do his word," His creation and my soul.

IN SUMMARY

We must guard our thoughts, our feelings and our wills, and bless and praise the Lord for who He is and what He has done. We must personalize this praise, give Him thanks in faith and receive God´s blessing and trust in Him and His Word.

There are many reasons to praise God that are good to remember: His work of salvation on the cross of Calvary, His forgiveness of our iniquities and His healing of the sicknesses of our souls and of our bodies, His redeeming us and flooding us constantly with His favors and mercies, His fulfilling our desires, and His renewal of our strength and vision, as He does for the eagles. We know also that He is just, He is a Father who Loves us; he is merciful. We should love Him, trust in Him, honor Him, serve Him and BLESS HIM!

For Meditation and Group Sharing

Psalm 103 and the devotional

1. According to parts of the psalm described in verses 1-5, what is God's motive for what He does?

2. Compare the actions mentioned in verses 1-5 with what the Father does in the parable of Luke 15:20-24, 32.

3. Someone said that:

    - **GRACE** is what is given to one who does not merit it, and
    - **MERCY** is what is not given to one who deserves: and
    - **JUSTICE** is giving what is deserved.

    Which verse or phrase in this psalm describes grace and mercy?

4. According to verses 11, 13, 17-18, what type of person receives certain benefits?

5. Related to compassion, with whom is God compared?

6. Recall and describe experiences in which you received mercy.

7. What does verse 19 have to do with the previous part of the psalm?

8. Write a “psalm” in which you bless the Lord. Make sure to personalize your praise (“I”, or “me”).

Giving Thanks for What You Receive From the Lord

Read Psalm 118:1-15

We all need to appreciate what we have instead of complaining about what we do not have to be happier. When we are grateful, we not only appreciate the one who gives us different things, but we appreciate more what we have, especially from the Lord. Ezra 3:10-12 (ESV) says,

> "And when the builders laid the foundation of the temple of the Lord, the priests in their vestments came forward with trumpets, and the Levites, the sons of Asaph, with cymbals, to praise the Lord, according to the directions of David king of Israel. And they sang responsively, praising and giving thanks to the Lord, 'For he is good, for his steadfast love endures forever toward Israel.' And all the people shouted with a great shout when they praised the Lord, because the foundation of the house of the Lord was laid... But many of the priests and Levites and heads of father' houses, old men who had seen the first house, wept with a loud voice when they saw the foundation of this house being laid, though many shouted aloud for joy."

When the Jews returned from exile, the first thing they did was build a temple and an altar to the Lord. They celebrated the Feast of Tabernacles, remembering the years they traveled through the desert with their tents, protected and trusting only in the God of Israel. When they were thankful and praised God, they were happy acknowledging the goodness and the great love of the eternal God that permitted them to return to His presence.

It is believed that Psalm 118 was written by King David and sung in Ezra 3:10-12. It is also believed that Jesus sang this psalm at the end of the feast of Passover. This psalm instructs us that the Lord's nature is good, and His love is forever. It affirms our need to take refuge or trust only in the Lord, who is the only Savior. The psalm also describes the advantages of using His holy name and rejoicing in Him, of knowing the door of righteousness and His salvation as well as deciding to experience His salvation by faith only in Him.

Reasons for thanking the Lord:

Praising the Lord also means giving Him thanks and acknowledging what He is: He is good, and His mercy and love are eternal. Our gratitude must be continuous for who He is and for what He has done for us when He came to save us, and for His promises in His Word. The style of Hebrew poetry used in this psalm consists of repetition which gives emphasis to the description and allows the reader to see things at different angles.

Testifying through his personal experience, the psalmist says that in his anguish or urgent need, he said a deep prayer or gave an invocation. God answered and set him free; He put him in a spacious place. Salvation includes liberation and preservation.

Hebrews 13:5-6 says that the Lord is in our favor, and He is with those who help us.

> "Keep your life free from love of money, and be content with what you have, for he has said, "I will never leave you or forsake you." So, we can confidently say, 'The Lord is my helper; I will not fear; what can man do to me?'"

He places his enemies as footstool for His feet.

He is the best refuge.

It is much better to trust in God and take refuge in Him, than to trust in man or in any mortal, however important they may be. The Lord is refuge here and in eternity.

His Name is victory in any conflict. The nations surrounded King David to destroy him, who said this felt like an attack of bees. But even though there may be conflict around us, in the name of Jesus we will be victorious.

Joy is the result of our salvation. The Lord is my strength and my song. "Glad songs of salvation are in the tents of the righteous". Nehemiah 8:10 says, "Do not be grieved, for the joy of the Lord is your strength."

Justification means to declare a sinner righteous by the merits of another. Romans 5:1 says: "Justified by faith we have peace with God through our Lord Jesus Christ."

Propitiation refers to the fact that God is completely satisfied with what Christ did for us on the cross, paying for our sins and transgressions.

Salvation is liberation, preservation, and complete ransom.

IN SUMMARY:

When we recognize what God is for us, that He has been and is good, and that His love and mercy are everlasting, all we can do is thank Him, trust in Him, and praise Him. No matter what our need is, we should ask Him from the heart and trust in the work of Jesus Christ on the cross for us. When we receive His justification, we will also receive joy and strength from His presence. It is much better to take refuge and to trust in God our Savior than in any man, no matter how important that man may be. God is the only one who loves us with eternal love and shows us mercy in all our needs, especially in our spiritual life. And as to His children, He has given us His name, the name of Jesus Christ, that brings victory, health, and salvation in any need.

For Meditation and Group Sharing

Psalm 118:1-15 and the devotional

1. The first words of this psalm are found in many passages of the Bible: The Lord is ____, and his ____

   _________________________".

   Psalm 106:9

   Psalm 107:1 (and compared with repeated verses)

   Psalm 136 (in every verse!)

   I Chronicles 16: 31 – 36, 41

   I Chronicles 5: (1, 5) 13 – 14

   Jeremiah 33: 11

2. In verse 7, "the Lord is for me… Who ____________________________

   ________________?"

   List people who have been "among those who help me".

3. Read verse 8. In which ways do people "trust in man"?

4. In what ways do people trust in people in authority, in high positions, politicians, among others (to get something)?

5. Read verse 13. "But the Lord..."

   It reminds us of Samson (Judges 16:23-30). On which famous occasion did he use the name of the Lord?

6. The people of Israel and the nation of Israel have experienced what the psalmist expresses in verse 10a, for example:

7. How have you experienced what verse 14 says?

8. Choose some verses from Psalm 118:1- 15 that encourage you and cheer you. Copy and repeat them.

A PSALM FOR THE BEGINNING OF THE YEAR

Read Psalm 118:16-29

We do not know exactly what will come—we can only guess—but we are confident because we are going with the Lord who knows the door, the way, and the end of the way. Every beginning is an opportunity to improve by making good decisions. The start of every year is an opportunity to sow with dreams and visions based on the promises and the love of God, and to harvest at the end of the year.

Jeremiah 29:11 (ESV) says: "For I know the plans I have for you, declares the Lord, plans for welfare and not for evil, to give you a future and a hope." Isaiah 41:10 (ESV) says: "Fear not, for I am with you; be not dismayed, for I am your God; I will strengthen you, I will help you, I will uphold you with my righteous right hand."

At the beginning of each year, we have an opportunity to prepare and to put things in order: for example, to purge our cell phones and our computers of what is not useful, to clear our souls of negative thoughts and negative sentiments from the past, to substitute these for the Word of God, and to start building new habits.

The Lord Himself is the motive for our security and happiness. He is our salvation and corrects us and makes us better in everything; He shows us the door and the correct way; He instructs us how to build our lives using the proper foundations and materials, how to be successful here and in eternity.

Let's start and finish with the attitude of gratitude, acknowledgement, and praise to the good God full of eternal love toward us. This is what King David is teaching us in the second part of Psalm 118.

A personal relationship with the Lord

We were created and redeemed to have fellowship with the Lord who strengthens us and gives us joy and happiness. He shows us His extraordinary power and victory amidst any need.

> "The Lord is my strength and my song; he has become my salvation. Glad songs of salvation are in the tents of the righteous; the right hand of the Lord does valiantly, the right hand of the Lord exalts, the right hand of the Lord does valiantly!" (from verses 14 – 16, ESV).

With His power, with His right hand, we have victory.

The Feast of Tabernacles is the commemoration of temporary, portable housing in the desert, which the Israelites lived in for forty years after being freed from slavery in Egypt. It is called *Sukot* in Hebrew and is during the harvest feast. It lasts seven days, is generally in September or October, and is characterized with exuberant joy. In our lives, the Lord is with us, including times of correction which are not for destruction but for improvement.

Rejection of acceptance

The only door of salvation is Jesus, and the only way to victory is Jesus, who justifies and preserves us, listens to our prayers, and responds to them. When we go through that door, we need to build an appropriate foundation using the proper materials. "The stone that the builders rejected has become the cornerstone. This is the Lord's doing; it is marvelous in our eyes."

The religious leaders rejected Jesus, His teaching, and His work, because of their pride, their religious zeal, and their lack of faith. They rejected the Lord because of His Galilean origin (John 7:52), for His lack of "formal religious education" (John 7:15), for not following their traditions (Luke 6:2), and for choosing sinners and publicans as His friends (Matthew 9:11). But the Lord who makes Himself known by revelation, does this in those who humble themselves, repent and believe in Him.

"But to those who receive Him, to those who believe in his name He gave them the right to become the children of God" (John 1:12). The invitation is, "Come to me all you that weary and heavy laden, and I will give you rest..." (Matthew 11:28). "So that at the name of Jesus every knee should bow, in heaven and on earth and under the earth" (Philippians 2:10 ESV).

To those who receive Him, God gives joy and happiness continually. When Jesus entered Jerusalem, the young people exclaimed: "Hosanna to the Son of David! Blessed is the one who comes in the name of the Lord." The psalm says, "This is the day that the Lord has made; we will rejoice and be glad in it. Save us [Hosanna}, we pray, O Lord! Blessed is he who comes in the name of the Lord. We bless you from the house of the Lord." All who call on the name of the Lord will be saved: complete salvation, complete liberation, blessed preservation and prosperity.

IN SUMMARY:

The Lord is the only God; He has given us the light of His Word to guide our way. We need to seize that truth, receiving by faith with gratitude and praise. The psalm ends the same way as it begins: giving thanks to the Lord for He is good and because His mercy endures forever.

For Meditation and Group Sharing

Psalm 118:15-29 and the above devotional

1. Have you ever been surrounded, either literally or spiritually, and were you able to rebuke those forces in the name of the Lord?

2. What warning did David give Goliath before he threw a rock? See I Samuel 17.

3. Describe a time when you were impressed by what someone told you about the "works of the Lord".

4. Recount times in which the Lord responded or surprised you, and it was evident that "this is of the Lord, admirable in our eyes" (verse 23).

5. From this psalm, list the roles that were fulfilled in Jesus:

    - Verse 22:

    - Verses 25-26:

6. What does the salvation of the Lord consist of? How have you seen this in your own life?

The Lord is Your Keeper

Read Psalm 121

Psalm 121 is written in the context of the Israelites on their pilgrimage walking toward Jerusalem—which is on a hill—and on the way, there are dangers. We are all on a pilgrimage in this temporary life and we are headed toward eternity. On our way we need security, and we often need help and assistance amidst diverse difficulties. Our difficulties or circumstances can be spiritual or physical, internal or external, so, we continually need help and protection. We need to lift our eyes to the solution, and God our Savior, Lord and Protector, always has the best solution.

The psalmist says in first person, "I lift up my eyes to the hills. From where does my help come? My help comes from the Lord who made heaven and earth."

Our focus should be on the solution and not on the problem. We should look up above us, not to the mountains, creation, creatures, or any other source of response. Not in any place either, but on the Lord who is the only Lord and Savior. Hebrews says 12:2 (ESV) says, "Looking to Jesus, the founder and perfecter of our faith".

The psalmist asks himself the question, "From where does my help come?". It should come from the Lord and Creator. Hebrews 4:16 says, "Let us then with confidence draw near to the throne of grace, that we may receive mercy and find grace to help in time of need." It speaks in the context of the work of

Jesus for us on the cross. Jeremiah 33:3 says: "Call unto me and I will answer you..."

The psalmist speaks (in second person) about nature and the characteristics of the Lord as Keeper and Protector as He was for Israel in their journey in the desert, which is remembered and celebrated in the Feast of Tabernacles, or *Sukot*.

God is your keeper, in Hebrew *shamarti*: guardian, one who keeps something that is valuable. He will not let your foot slip. He will not go to sleep. The road in life has its risks, and to avoid falling, we need protection and help. Jude verse 24 (ESV) says, "To him who is able to keep you from stumbling and to present you blameless before the presence of his glory with great joy..." *Adonai*, my Lord, who keeps us never tires or sleeps and takes care of us, sees everything, knows everything, loves us and has promises for us. We should involve the Lord in all the aspects of our lives, in every place, time and circumstance.

"The Lord is your shade on your right hand." This hand represents power, and the shade is the protection of the Lord everywhere, even though sometimes we do not see it. The sun with its heat during the day does not affect us. Like Israel in the desert, we need the cloud in the day, and the column of fire at night to dissipate fear and cold.

"He will keep you from all evil." He will keep our whole being (3 John 2 and I Thessalonians 5:23). Exodus 12:13 says, "When I see the blood, I will pass over you (I will keep you)". Romans 8:38, 39 says nothing "will be able to separate us from the love of God that is in Christ Jesus our Lord." In John 10:10, Jesus said, "I have come that you might have life and have it abundantly."

"The Lord will keep your going out and your coming in from this time forth and forevermore," from your house, your work, activities, trips, projects and everywhere in the pilgrimage of life, from youth and maturity to eternity.

IN SUMMARY:

Philippians 4:6 says: "Be not anxious about anything, but in everything by prayer and supplication with thanksgiving let your requests be made known to God." It would be so good to evaluate ourselves and ask, with our eyes upward, "Where does my help come from?" Does it come from the Lord Creator"? Only the Lord God through Jesus Christ can help us and protect us; He is the Creator and Savior. Let us see and accept the true guardian of our souls; let us believe and trust in Him.

AMEN

For Meditation and Group Sharing

Psalm 121 and the above devotional

1. Throughout the history of mankind, in different cultures (including Israel) it was common to practice idolatry on the hills. God warned Israel constantly to not do this (2 Kings 14:3-4). The idols were not removed and the people offered sacrifices and burned incense to them in the high places. Nowadays, to which things, people, or places, do people who do not seek God look, wanting to find relief and tranquility? Read Psalm 115 and comment.

2. Read verse 3. Imagine a guard who goes to sleep; what can easily happen to a person or place under his responsibility?

3. Read Psalm 66:7 and 9 (ESV), "His eyes keep watch over the nations... who has kept our soul among the living and has not let our feet slip." Compare this passage with verse 3 and record your thoughts.

4. Thinking about possible dangers when you are on foot or in a vehicle, in temptations or in the confusion that ideologies bring, how can you express what the Lord does and who He is for you?

5. Inspired by this psalm, and based on what the Lord has done, write to another person telling them what He will do for him or her.

Counsel for Parents

Read Psalm 127

Psalm 127 is the counsel of God and His Word to positively impact the futures of children and society.

In our lives, edification is essential, not only in the physical, but also in the spiritual and eternal. This depends largely on our development in childhood, as we see in this psalm. Home is a place where lives are molded for the future. In His Word, God proposes that we let Him be the Builder, in order to obtain good results in our homes and families. Life, family, and children are only temporarily in the home. Children are a gift from God. While they are in our care, we are to influence them and send them off into the future like arrows, so that they bear good fruit that lasts both here and in eternity.

Build and keep

These two functions are so important; if God does not do them, they are done in vain. Building homes and families with principles and the values of love and righteousness, and keeping God in the forefront will give us a better future. Matthew 6:33 says, "Seek first the kingdom of God and his righteousness, and all these things will be added to you."

To build is to cultivate with purposes and goals. To keep these, we must defend them and guard them constantly. In Genesis 2:15, God gave Adam duties in the garden of Eden to cultivate it and guard it. These activities were performed in an atmosphere full of the presence of God, and with delight and pleasure (the meaning of "Eden"). In Nehemiah 4:17, we see that during the rebuilding of the Jerusalem wall, men carried a load on their backs, with one hand working and a weapon in the other to defend themselves from enemies. To restore our homes, with God and His Word, we must dedicate time to instruct and disciple our children. In the Hebrew language the words "work", "serve", and "worship" have the same root.

Children are a gift of God

Hard work is very important for survival, but it is also important to rest daily, trusting in the Lord who gives us everything. He gives us a job, peace, love, and provision. We must dedicate time to be with our children and to provide biblical instruction at their level.

We should acknowledge that God gives us children as a gift that we are not only to take care of, but also to prepare for the future. Children are in the home (the quiver) temporarily. During that time, we are to prepare them with love, value, and purpose and to launch them into life using the tools God has given as we have fellowship with Him and with His Word. This prepares them for any future situation.

In Matthew 7:24 (ESV), Jesus says, "He that hears my words and does them I will compare to a wise man who builds his house on the rock; the floods came, and the winds blew and beat on that house, but it did not fall, because it had been founded on the rock."

Children should be prepared with purpose:

To be successful in life, based on eternal values and with love, children should be oriented and instructed in the Word of God, launched like arrows, with value, to reach a target in life. They should be prepared to reach spiritual and emotional stability in everything, according to their aptitudes, talents, and gifts from God. Instead of producing shame, they will be the reason for parental pride and will contribute to improving society.

IN SUMMARY:

Our children are a gift from God and through them, we are given an opportunity to build lives. We should invite God through Jesus Christ, the only mediator between God and man, to be part of this process. We must decide to study the Word of God and apply it as a principal tool with the defined purpose of bettering our children's futures.

For Meditation and Group Sharing

Psalm 127 and the above devotional

According to a note in the subtitle, this psalm is from David's son, Solomon. We are not told in which season of his life he wrote it, but it was written by the inspiration of the Holy Spirit.

1. How would you rewrite verse 1 in the affirmative instead of the negative?

2. What does the psalmist say is "in vain" in verse 2?

3. Is it wrong to get up early and go to bed late?

4. The word "anxious" changes everything. Worry, anxiety, and fear about tomorrow demonstrate a lack of faith in God. It is important to take enough time to rest well at night. Jesus spoke clearly about that, as we see in Matthew 6. What type of atmosphere is created in the home and family when there is worry, lack of sleep and no faith in the Lord, and what does this teach children?

5. In verse 1, as we read the words "house" and "city", think about people. Based on this verse, who do we need when we build our homes and societies, and why?

6. In verse 5, the passage mentions “the gate” of the city where the authorities and leaders would talk, and where they made important decisions. According to this verse, it could also be a place to talk with enemies. What kinds of things would a person hear from their enemy that may shame them as parents?

7. Who or what are the enemies of our children?

8. If the Lord has been the Counselor and Guardian for the parents, what will happen to their enemies?

From My Mother's Womb You Have Taken Me Into Account

Read Psalm 139

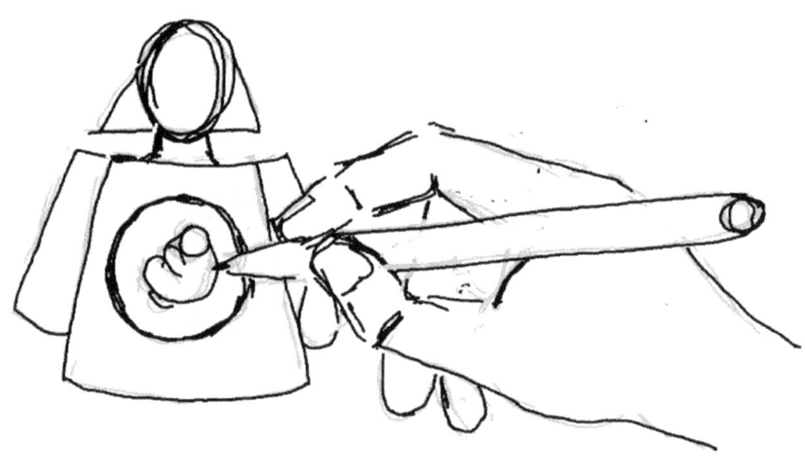

In this psalm, David, in a very personal way, refers to the greatness of the creator God: omniscient, omnipresent, omnipotent. He not only knows all things profoundly, but He knows us and He is very interested in us individually. He has a design for each life, a plan, and a purpose from before birth; from conception and throughout our entire lives. But He is also a holy God who abhors evil. We should be on His side and hate sin but love the sinner. We should also ask God to examine us and show us our sins, and we should let Him guide us and be forgiven by Jesus Christ who died for us.

God knows me and protects me

In this psalm, David tells us about a personal and loving God saying that the Lord has examined us and has known us. Before Him we are like a transparent window. He knows our thoughts before we speak them, and He knows our rising and our resting. To bless us, He loves us and protects us constantly as if there were a guard around us.

When David was anointed to be king in front of his brothers, God saw his inner being.

He is everywhere

God the Holy Spirit is in all places in heaven and on earth, even in Seol as judge and owner. We cannot escape from His presence. He is everywhere, even in the darkest place, and we cannot hide anything from Him. "If we confess our sins, He is faithful and just to forgive our sins, and to cleanse us from all unrighteousness [iniquity]" (I John 1:9).

Our Body

Our bodies are formed by God from conception until birth, and He has a design, a plan and a purpose for life; we are formed in the depth of the womb and wonderfully made, for example, the muscles, veins, arteries and nerves, and all the rest. David says, "My soul knows it very well," acknowledging with all certainty that God has formed us, even from embryogenesis.

God says to the prophet Jeremiah (1:5), "Before I formed you in the womb I knew you, and before you were born, I consecrated you, I appointed you a prophet to the nations." God has a defined plan and a purpose for each one from the beginning, even before being formed in the womb. He loves us from our beginning and now, and for this reason, He gave His Son on the cross so that each one could have eternal life believing in Him.

If our physical bodies are so important to God and His purpose in this life, of even more importance is our eternal destiny after this life. We should respect our bodies and defend them from the beginning of their formation and manage them well during life.

The wicked before God

Seeing the innumerable wonders of God when He formed us from the beginning, and His thoughts, purposes, and plans for us, we should receive His plan for our lives and bless His holy name. God Himself called those who reject His love and His plan wicked and ungodly. They deserve spiritual death and condemnation for opposing and rebelling against His goodness. John 3:18 says, "He who believes in Him is not condemned [judged]; but he who does not believe, is condemned already because he has not believed in the name of the only begotten Son of God."

IN SUMMARY

Let's pray with David, "Search me, O God, and know my heart. Try me and know my thoughts! And see if there be any grievous way in me and lead me in the way everlasting!"

"Let us draw near in confidence before the throne of grace to obtain mercy and find grace for the opportune help." **AMEN.**

For Meditation and Group Sharing

Read Psalm 139 and the above devotional

1. Make a drawing that represents what verse 5 says, and draw yourself as you are today.

2. In verse 7, David speaks about the Spirit of God. Read I Samuel 16:13 and Psalm 51:7-11 and describe the relationship between the Spirit and David.

3. Read verse 9 in the Modern English paraphrase. For David, which sea was to the west?

4. How do you respond when you meditate on verses 13-16, that God formed you from conception?

5. Express a praise to God for the way He formed you.

6. Between verses 22 and 23, it seems that David reflected on his attitude toward the wicked, perverse and "men of blood". He suddenly stops and asks God to examine his heart. Comment on this.

7. Choose a verse from verses 1-6 to copy and remember.

“Come Let Us Reason Together,” Says the Lord.

Read Isaiah 1

Isaiah is the longest book of the major prophets in the Old Testament, and it is the book most mentioned in the New Testament, especially in the gospels. It is a book of prophecy containing poetry that encourages us and gives us strength with its resources of faith and hope, offering inner and physical healing.

The prophet Isaiah prophesied between the years 745 and 695 B.C., during the reigns of Jotham, Ahaz and Hezekiah. Isaiah was cousin to King Uzziah and informed about the politics and problems of that time.

In that era, Israel was divided into two kingdoms; a southern kingdom consisting of Judah and Benjamin, with its capital in Jerusalem, and a northern kingdom made up of the rest of the tribes, with its capital in Samaria. The northern kingdom had recently been conquered by Assyria due to disobedience to the Lord and for having left His commandments. Isaiah now prophesies and warns Judah and Jerusalem not to fall into the same trap.

The message is directed to a corrupt society separated from divine values, but with religion and external liturgy. The Lord shows them their sin and proposes repentance to cleanse and restore them.

Charges against Judah and Jerusalem:

Initially Isaiah mentions the witnesses, heaven and earth, who, in Deuteronomy 30:19, witnessed the beginning of Isreal’s history.

In Judah and Jerusalem, there was a lack of acknowledgement of the lordship of God or that He sustained them, in contrast to the ox and the donkey who knew their master. Judah and Jerusalem did not acknowledge the care and prosperity that the Lord had given them.

Then, due to the rebellion of their hearts, they fell into iniquity, being a wicked generation; not just those in government, but all society, with corruption (abuse of power), and permitted bribes, idolatry, and injustice against widows and orphans. This sin brought desolation to the land, imminent punishment, and complete internal sickness. Only a faithful remnant of the city and the population had not been destroyed, similar to what happened with Sodom and Gomorrah.

Worst was that they did not acknowledge their sin before the Lord, and they went on with the same external religiosity, their hearts far from Him, and with outright rebellion to the holy spiritual principles of the Lord. Isaiah speaks to the leaders of the people and calls them "princes of Sodom and people of Gomorrah," associating them with the degrading sins of those cities that were destroyed as an example.

Their religion was intensified on the outside with sacrifices, offerings and prayers or good works. But if their attitudes and conduct did not change, Isaiah 64:6 said, they are like filthy rags (contaminated garments) before the Lord. "Unless the Lord builds the house, those who build it labor in vain" (Psalm 127:1). If we evaluated our internal relationship with God, and our religion and works, how would we measure up?

Last opportunity: "Come and let us reason together":

They, and all who have the same problem, needed to be cleansed and to stop doing evil before the eyes of the Lord, to learn to do good, practice justice, stop oppressing others and defend the widow and the orphan.

How is that done?

First, this is achieved by coming to the Lord and turning from evil ways (this is repentance).

"Come now" is an invitation to make an urgent decision, not leave it for later.

"Reason" is to use the mind to change, repenting, to be clean; if the sins are red or crimson, the robes will be white as snow and like wool.

"If we confess our sins, he is faithful and just to forgive us our sins and to cleanse us from all unrighteousness (I John 1:9).

"Come to me all you that labor and are heavy laden, and I will give you rest" (Matthew 11:28).

For all social, family, and individual corruption, there is only one solution: repent and come to the Lord and receive forgiveness through the sacrifice of the One who took our sins on the cross, the Lord Jesus Christ. Then we must acknowledge Him as Lord and enter a discipleship to learn about Him and to be transformed. This is the only way to have individual, family, and social restoration. The alternative is to reject the love and forgiveness of God, which will bring emptiness, shame, and destruction.

Acts 2:38 says, "Repent and be baptized each one of you in the name of Jesus Christ for the forgiveness of your sins, and you will receive the gift of the Holy Spirit."

And Romans 12:1 - 2 says,

> "I beseech you, therefore, brethren, by the mercies of God, that you present your bodies a living sacrifice, holy and acceptable to Him, which is your reasonable service. And be not conformed to this world, but be transformed by the renewing of your mind, that you may prove what is the good and acceptable and perfect will of God."

For Meditation and Group Sharing

Isaiah 1 and the above devotional

1. In general, why did the prophet write this book (according to the devotional)?

2. List the great sins of God´s people mentioned in Isaiah 1.

3. What were the consequences?

4. Do you think there are consequences today for certain sins? Explain.

5. What is the worst part about having sin?

6. Then and today, what are some good religious works that in themselves do not make people pleasing to God?

7. In a nutshell, what pleases God is:

8. What did the leaders and the people have to do?

9. What similarities do you see in our times?

10. What is the process of learning in our walk with the Lord?

11. Describe the stages, if you have had them, of your learning process.

12. Can you identify signs of corruption in your own heart, in your family, or in your circle of friends, work and others?

13. After identifying these, what should follow next?

14. What is your prayer regarding this meditation?

A Vision and a Call From God

Read Isaiah 6

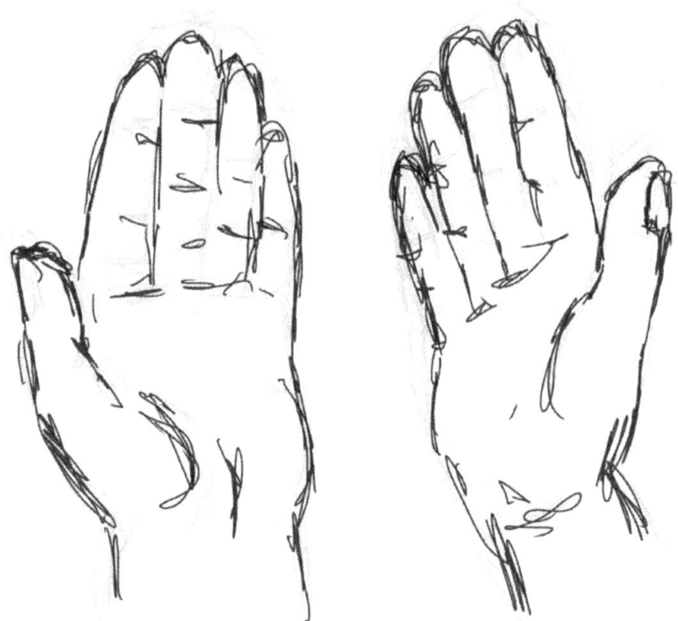

Worship and praise to God for knowing Him as He is, prepares us for service so we can fulfill the purpose for which we are called. Worship and praise is an expression of the greatness and the holiness of the Lord, as well as providing a way to be cleansed and prepared for Him to fulfill His purpose in our lives. Chapter 5 of Isaiah describes God as a vine dresser who planted a vineyard and took care of it so it would bear grapes; but it gave wild grapes. The vine refers to Judah and Jerusalem.

In the year Isaiah was called to be a prophet, King Uzziah died. Uzziah had been a good king during most of his life, and so for his obedience and fear of the Lord, he prospered financially, militarily and in everything. But in his abundance, he became proud, and in his pride, he burned incense in the temple of the Lord, which only the high priest was allowed to do. While he was inside doing this, he was rebuked by the priests, but he got angry, and the Lord, in his anger, struck him with leprosy. Uzziah had to be pulled out of the temple quickly, and he remained isolated in his house until his death.

In this context of seeing the holiness and justice of the Lord, Isaiah had a vision. God is love, but He is also a consuming fire. Isaiah had a personal experience with the majesty and holiness of the Lord; he was called by God for a specific function evidenced by what happened later.

The personal encounter with God and his holiness:

Isaiah describes his vision in first person. He had just lost his cousin, King Uzziah, but he saw the Lord God seated on His throne, high and sublime. He saw seraphim, who are angels of high rank, carrying out the highest function: praising and worshiping the Lord. They said to each other: "Holy, holy, holy is the Lord of hosts; the earth is full of his glory." When he perceived the glory of the triune God and saw the seraphim humbly covering their faces and feet and serving the Lord, Isaiah felt like a sinner. With humility, he recognized that he was a sinner and said, "Woe is me! For I am lost; for I am a man of unclean lips, and I dwell amidst a people of unclean lips..."

Isaiah was a just man, but when he perceived the majesty and the holiness of God, he recognized himself as a sinner. In that moment, one of the seraphim took tongs in his hand and picked up a burning coal from the altar to touch his mouth to cleanse his sin.

We now receive forgiveness and purification of our sins from the cross of Christ when we acknowledge the greatness and the holiness of God, and believe, by faith, in the work of the cross. We then submit to His will so that He may place us, call us, and send us in His specific purpose.

Have you acknowledged the majesty and the lordship of God? Have you recognized the need for forgiveness and cleansing of your heart and your mouth? Have you accepted with faith and humility the work of God's judgment that fell on the Lord Jesus Christ on the cross?

The call

When Isaiah confessed his sin, he was forgiven and cleansed by grace and by faith, and he was prepared to listen to the Lord. "Whom will I send and who will go for us?" the triune God asked. Isaiah answered, with humility, willingness, and submission to the will of the Lord, "Here am I, send me."

When we have the personal experience of salvation and forgiveness of sins by grace through faith, we are ready to be sent. God sends volunteers that respond to His call. Would you be willing to go?

The specific function

The specific message that Isaiah had to give was of repentance to a rebellious people that did not understand what it heard, that did not comprehend what it saw, and whose hearts were insensitive.

John 12:40-41 applies the same words of Isaiah to the Pharisees who rejected the words of Christ. This passage also refers to Jesus, whom Isaiah saw here on his throne. Due to their lack of sensitivity and faith, Jesus spoke to the people in parables, to receive the Word and repent of their sins.

Isaiah asked: "How long, O Lord?" How long will the people be rebellious? The Lord said it would be until the people suffered the consequences of desolation and dispersion; however, hope is the remnant that remains as holy seed in a trunk that has been cut.

Are you among the remnant? If so, we should prepare our hearts with an appropriate attitude, our ears with attention, and our spiritual eyes perceiving what the Word of God says.

All of us need a personal encounter with God, with His holiness, and His lordship, recognizing our sins. As sinners, it is normal to feel small, with the need to receive forgiveness and cleansing by grace through faith. It is only through the work of the One who paid for us on the cross, to justify us and sanctify us. Once we have that encounter, we must voluntarily offer ourselves for the Lord to fulfill His purpose in our lives. We must also prepare our hearts with willingness, as well as our eyes to see and ears to listen, to receive and obey the Word of God. As a result, we bear fruit in the Word that God has entrusted to us, like Isaiah, who, even though only a remnant, received the message in his time. Through him, almost 2,700 years later, many of us have received the message and believed the Word of God.

For Meditation and Group Sharing

Isaiah 6 and the above devotional:

1. Describe what Isaiah saw in a vision from God.

2. What differences are there between the attitude of the people of Judah described in Chapter 1 and the attitude of Isaiah in Chapter 6?

3. How did what Isaiah saw from God have to do with how he saw himself?

4. Compare the condition of the people to whom God sent Isaiah, with the condition of many today.

5. Explain your responses to the three questions in the middle of the comment:

- Have you acknowledged the majesty and lordship of God?

- Have you perceived the need for forgiveness and cleansing in your heart and in your mouth?

- Have you accepted by faith and humility the work of God's judgment that fell on the Lord Jesus Christ on the cross?

6. What must one do to for "the remnant" to grow today?

7. What relationship have you found between internal cleansing and your calling?

The Humanity and Divinity of the Messiah

Read Isaiah 7:14 and 9:6

The birth of the Messiah was a miraculous sign, and His names wonderfully give us not only His character and function, but also His divine and human nature.

In Chapter 1 of the book of the prophet Isaiah, we saw our need to settle accounts and make an evaluation of our relationship with God, as well as the need to change our route toward Him, and change our way of thinking to be forgiven and cleansed by Him.

In Chapter 6 we saw the prophet Isaiah in a personal encounter with God the Lord, majestic and holy. Isaiah acknowledged himself as a sinner and was cleansed by a burning coal that came from the altar. It prepared and sanctified him by faith and by grace to fulfill his ministry.

The Messiah Savior

In Isaiah 7:14, a prophecy is a sign with two fulfillments: one in the time of King Ahaz, and another 700 years later with the birth of the Messiah, mentioned in Matthew 1:21. In Isaiah, the prophet refers to a sign that is a miracle of God. "The virgin will conceive and bear a son, and shall call his name Immanuel" (God with us). Not only would God be with that son who would be born, but He would be God Himself; and He would also be man born of a woman; a virgin, giving birth supernaturally.

In Matthew 1:21 we see the angel Gabriel who appeared in dreams to Joseph who was betrothed to Mary (there were three stages: commitment, betrothal, and marriage) to announce that he should not be afraid to take Mary as his wife, because what was conceived in her was of the Holy Spirit. And in the same dream, he was given the name Jesus (*Yeshua* or *Yehoshua*— "The Lord saves"), for the child who would be born "shall save his people from their sins."

For Joseph, as a descendant of King David, it was the fulfillment of prophecy to King Ahaz in Isaiah 7:12. He received by revelation the knowledge of the nature of the Messiah who would be born: divine, to be conceived by the Holy Spirit and thus without sin, and human as descendant of David through his mother Mary. As a human he identified with the fallen human race and with sinners in his lineage (see Matthew Chapter 1), and He ate with sinners, called sinners as His disciples, and was crucified between two sinners.

To know Jesus as the Messiah, it is necessary to have this knowledge by revelation.

Matthew 16:16 says that Jesus asked his disciples who people said He was, then He asked them: Who do you say that I am?

Peter responded: "You are the Christ, the Son of the living God."

Jesus said to him: "Blessed are you, Simon..., for flesh and blood has not revealed this to you, but my Father who is in heaven."

When Jesus was born, not everyone realized who He was, only those who had had the revelation from God.

- To the shepherds, an angel appeared to announce the birth of "a Savior who is Christ the Lord," with a sign to find the child.
- The Holy Spirit revealed to Simeon and Anna, two elderly people who arrived at the temple, that the child being presented was the Messiah.
- God showed the men who came from the east a star to show the place where "the King of the Jews" was born.

Have you had or asked God for the revelation of that Savior and Lord?

The Messiah Lord

We read in Isaiah 9:1 that for the regions north of the kingdom of Israel and near Galilea by the area of the Gentiles there is a hope of salvation and of seeing the light. This prophecy was fulfilled when Jesus started His ministry, as described by Matthew (4:13-17).

"The Lord Jesus is the light that gives light to everyone, coming to this world; the light of this world and he that follows Me will not walk in darkness, but will have the light of life" (John 8:12).

The names of the Messiah, according to Isaiah 9:6, are characteristics of the Messiah and show us His human-divine nature as King and Lord.

- "For to us a child is born, to us a son is given." He is a child born as a human, but He is given as Son by God.

  "For God so loved the world, that He gave His only begotten Son, that whoever believes in Him should not perish, but have everlasting life" (John 3:16).
- "And the government shall be upon his shoulder." He carries on Himself lordship and majesty; he is King of kings and Lord of lords.
- He is "wonderful Counselor, mighty God, everlasting Father." He is God worthy of worship and praise.

  Hebrews 1:8 refers to Him: "Your throne, O God, is forever and ever."
- He is the Almighty; Matthew 28:18 says: "All power has been given to me in heaven and in earth; therefore, go make disciples..."

  The Lord Jesus has been given the name above all names that are named (Ephesians 1:21), the highest name (Philippians 2:9-11).
- He is the "Prince of Peace". He has made peace between God and man; he justifies us by faith when we receive Him by faith and acknowledge Him as Lord in our lives.

The miraculous birth of the Messiah was prophesied 700 years before by the prophet Isaiah. It is a sign for everyone. His nature—totally human and divine—to be our perfect Savior and Lord, the One who took our place dying as a Lamb, to liberate us and make us part of His kingdom. When He rose from the dead, he was given the name above all names, and now he is at the Father´s right hand interceding for us as High Priest.

He is our Counsellor, our Mighty Helper and the only One who gives us true peace.

Do you need peace? Come now to the Prince of Peace, Jesus Christ.

Do you have a situation that robs you of peace? Philippians 4:6, 7 (ESV) says,

> "Do not be anxious about anything, but in everything by prayer and supplication with thanksgiving, let your requests be made known to God. And the peace of God, which surpasses all understanding, will guard your hearts and your minds in Christ Jesus."

For Meditation and Group Sharing

Isaiah 7:4 and 9:6 and the above devotional

1. Who is Jesus, according to the fulfillment of Isaiah 7:14?

2. Why is it significant that He was conceived by a virgin?

3. Who is Jesus, according to the fulfillment of Isaiah 9:6?

4. The angel Gabriel´s message to Joseph was very important. Why?

5. The angel spoke to him of the name and the mission of the Son; what were they?

6. Before that, Gabriel visited Mary (see Luke 1:26–38). How did he describe the child who would be conceived?

7. Read Isaiah 9:6.
   - What counsel has the Lord Jesus given to you?
   - How has He shown you His power?

8. What has he shown you about God the Father?

9. How has He brought you peace?

10. Maybe today the Lord Jesus is asking you, “Who do you say that I am?” By revelation of what you have heard, read, meditated or received, what is your response?

11. How can you respond to God as you contemplate these two prophecies of Isaiah and the fulfillment in Jesus?

HEZEKIAH'S HEALING
Read Isaiah 38

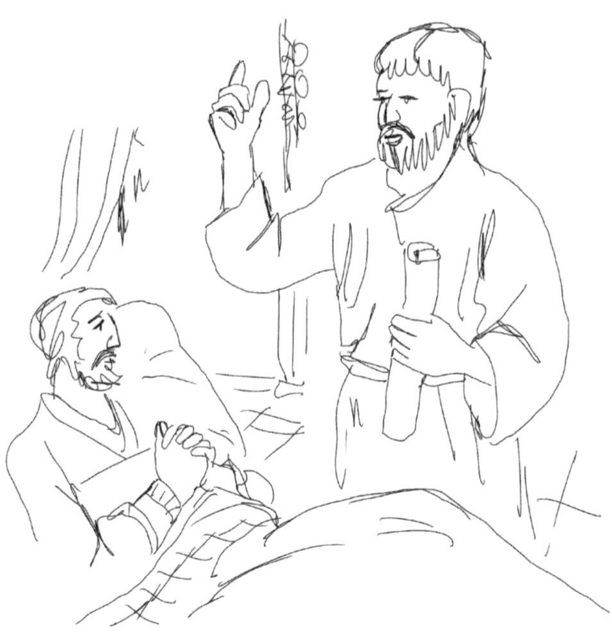

Problems and difficulties can be a great opportunity to experience miracles and to know God better. The first part of Isaiah 38 refers to the serious sickness of King Hezekiah and how he was healed. The second part is a psalm of Hezekiah, king of Judah, which expresses how he was emotionally and physically affected and what his attitude was when he was healed.

The name "Hezekiah" in Hebrew means "the Lord has strengthened" and was exactly what Hezekiah needed and experienced. In those days, his territory was in imminent danger of invasion by Sennacherib, king of Assyria. Also, he became seriously ill.

As an important personal record, Hezekiah did restoration in the temple of the Lord: he cleaned it of idolatry, destroyed the bronze serpent that Moses had made in the desert, which was at that time an object of worship, and established worship only to God.

King Hezekiah became very ill at about 39 years of age, and the prophet Isaiah came to announce to him, "Set your house in order, for you shall die, you shall not recover."

God in sovereignty decides the days of human life and waits for us, meanwhile, to set our things and our houses in order. The sickness affected not only King Hezekiah's physical body, but also his mental and emotional state. But when he came to God according to His Word and with a correct attitude, Hezekiah was healed and strengthened. The result is a testimony that benefits others.

The first part of Hezekiah's song

In this part of the psalm, Hezekiah describes sincere feelings of frustration, discouragement, and negative thoughts for not having prepared to die, and discouragement upon knowing all he was going to lose, especially the opportunity to praise and worship the Lord in life. He finally remembers God in a fervent prayer.

Hezekiah's prayer

When, through Isaiah, he heard the Word of the Lord and that he was going to die, Hezekiah prayed. He did not turn to anybody else here on earth or in heaven, but only to the Lord. He prayed with humility and cried out from his innermost being.

Jeremiah 33:3 says: "Call to me and I will answer you..."

In his prayer, he remembered his restoration and worshipped sincerely before the Lord. James 5:15,16 says, "Confess your faults one to another, and pray for one another that you will be healed. The effectual fervent prayer of a righteousness man avails much." He asked for healing in his prayer with tears (v. 16).

According to the book of Kings, he was heard immediately. Isaiah was still on the patio of the royal house when the Lord sent him back with a word of healing.

The answer to prayer

The Lord saw Hezekiah's tears and heard his prayer, He remembered the covenant made with his ancestor David, and said He would add 15 years of life, with the promise that if in three days Hezekiah would go to the temple (this is in the book of Kings), that he and people of Judah would be freed from the king of Assyria.

When God gives life, He gives it with a plan and a purpose. Have you prayed for your needs with the attitude of Hezekiah? Are you willing to glorify God so that God's purpose in your life will be fulfilled? Have you trusted in the name of Jesus? In John 14:14, Jesus said, "If anyone asks anything in my name, I will do it." And according to Romans 8:26, we have the help and strength of the Holy Spirit when we let Him guide us and we pray.

A miraculous sign and the cake of figs

God, in his eternal love and faithfulness, strengthened Hezekiah's faith. He turned the shadow of the sun clock back the equivalent of 40 minutes and He told Hezekiah he would go to the temple in three days. Isaiah sent for Hezekiah to apply a "cake of figs" on the area of his sickness, and he was healed.

The Lord heals with or without help—as John Wesley said, using medical means or without them. It is important to acknowledge Him in first place as Sovereign and Lord, and to acknowledge that there is a purpose for living—to please God and to serve our neighbor.

At the end of King Hezekiah's psalm (verses 17-20), he mentions first the forgiveness of sins, then the need to give thanks to the Lord who is faithful in this earthly light, and to teach the future generations to do the same.

Salvation and liberation come through the merits and the work of Christ on the cross and are a gift of God. We must acknowledge Jesus as Lord, humble ourselves, and surrender to Him in worship in all the aspects of life, as Hezekiah did, praying with fervor in every need.

Have you considered the need of putting God in first place in your life? And of believing in the healing and liberating name of Jesus Christ and receiving of His mercy?

For Meditation and Group Sharing

Isaiah 8 and the above devotional:

1. Often in the Bible, the word "house" more refers more to family. What could be some of the family issues of a king that he would have to put in order?

2. God sent Isaiah to the king two times with messages. If Isaiah had not heard the second message, what would have been different?

3. Let´s remember that God sent Abraham to offer his son as a burnt sacrifice. Afterward, He spoke to him again and that changed everything. It is necessary that the messenger hear both times and that the listener hear both times. Has God spoken to you once and then again with a different message (for you or for another person)?

4. Why do you think that God added the sign of the sun?

5. In verse 12, the king compares his life with a woven work on the loom that God has not finished, and He cuts it off. Comment on this.

6. In verse 16, "And you will restore me to health and make me live" (literally), we see faith in the plea. Explain.

7. Verse 17 describes what, in addition to the healing, happened to him. Why do you think that Isaiah gave instruction to apply a mass of figs to the boil, after God assured him he had been heard?

8. Comment on verse 19.

9. If you have a health issue that needs healing, you can express it to God today with faith and hope and with an attitude of obedience.

The Comfort of God and How to Receive It

Read Isaiah 40:1-11

The comfort or the strength of God is good news that gives us security and hope, not only in the coming life, but especially in these moments we are living. Chapter 40 of Isaiah refers to the comfort of the Lord for His people Judah and Jerusalem. It refers also to the listeners of John the Baptist and to us today. The verb "comfort" as written is an imperative that implies action—there is an attitude and preparation that we must show to receive the good news, the promise of the faithful and powerful God.

Preparation refers to our change of direction and our way of thinking, which will have the positive result of receiving the good news of salvation. Our decisions determine the outcome and prepare us to be able to have a divine visitation today, and to receive Him in His coming as King, God, and Lord.

The good news that comforts

The good news is in the context of the love of God speaking to the heart of His people. Comfort is the result of two events: the Lord is coming as Savior and liberator, and the punishment of sin has been paid in full. Jesus in His first coming as Lamb came to take away the sin of the world. On the cross He took the wrath of justice because of our sins.

Preparation

Receiving the good news is like receiving the coming of a king for whom we must prepare the way. In this case, it is in our inner being, the heart, where we must remove obstacles. There is an announcement with big letters in the four gospels, "Repent, for the kingdom of heaven is at hand [has come near]," alluding to the preaching of John the Baptist who prepared the way for the Lord Jesus Christ. The repentance we need to experience consists of a change from our own way to the way of the Lord and with Him, and in our way of thinking. This should show fruits worthy of repentance.

This preparation is to receive the incorruptible seed of the Word of God. I Peter 1:23-25 (ESV) says,

> "You have been born again not of perishable seed but of imperishable, through the living and abiding word of God; for 'All flesh is like grass and all its glory like the flower of grass. The grass withers, and the flower falls, but the word of the Lord remains forever.' And this word is the good news that was preached to you."

We must prepare our hearts and remove all obstacles, all formalism and religiosity, unbelief, and pride. Those that are proud must humble themselves and those that have low self-esteem must accept the love of the Lord.

Decision

There is an invitation to decide to receive the Word of God and believe it, instead of following the desires of the carnal mind. When we prepare ourselves through repentance, glory is manifested, and the presence or the salvation of God to humanity; there we are choosing the message of salvation instead of our own selfish ways.

This is what God has said and planned, and this is what brings victory and success for all who believe.

Confidence in people, religion, and confidence in oneself to be saved, is like grass and its glory like the flower that dries and falls. The human mind without God is corrupt, and its best effort is in vain to obtain justification before God.

Only through the Word of God, when it is received and believed, are we born again to new life. Only Christ with His work for us is sufficient to save us and to bless us. Only the Spirit of the Lord gives us victory and comfort when we submit to Him. All flesh is like grass and its glory like the flower of the grass, but the Word of God abides forever.

The Word of the Lord has never been destroyed, despite persecution over time, and it has always remained because it is the Word of God.

The decision must be to see only our God, and the message must be given with strength, out loud and without fear, to all. "Turn to me and be saved, all the ends of the earth! For I am God, and there is no other" (Isaiah 45:22, ESV).

"For there is one God, and one mediator between God and man, the man Christ Jesus" (I Timothy 2:5). It is a call to decide to see only God—no thing or created being, no building, no human being, no goods, no representation—only the Creator.

The Lord will come to govern with power, with His rewards according to what we His people have done. Revelation 22:12 says, "Behold, I am coming soon, bringing my recompense with me, to repay each one for what he has done."

He will come as King and Lord, but now He is the Good Shepherd and calls each one by name (John 10:10-15); He is the Great Shepherd (Hebrews 13:20); He is the Prince of Shepherds (I Peter 5:4). He will separate the sheep from the goats (Matthew 25:31 - 33). He will come as judge and king, but now He is Savior and Lord. We must listen with attention to the message of good news, receive it and believe it, prepare our hearts, remove all obstacles, and turn to God and accept Him our Shepherd today.

For Meditation and Group Sharing

Isaiah 40:1-11 and the above devotional

1. What is the comfort in verse 1?

2. In ancient times, a road was prepared where a king would come. Explain verses 3 and 4 in terms of God´s people and the imminent coming of King Jesus.

3. What does "the word of the Lord abides forever" mean?

4. It is God´s desire "to reveal His glory". Jesus said it in His prayer in John 17: 22,24. What does this refer to?

5. Contrast "the glory of man" with "the glory of the Lord".

6. In verse 9, God said to "Jerusalen, herald of good news", to raise its voice without fear, saying to the cities: "Here is your God". How does this apply to us?

7. Verse 10 reminds us of Isaiah 6 (previous topic). Research and explain "the government" and "the reward" that the Lord will have after He comes for His own.

8. Explain verse 11, from figurative language to what the Lord Jesus does with us.

9. Express now the comfort of the Lord that brings knowing and trusting in His grace, glory, government, and reward.

STRENGTH LIKE THE EAGLES'

Read Isaiah 40:12-31

Like Israel in exile, even God's people can go through difficult situations and experience weakness, fatigue, and insecurity. And, like Israel, we also need to know what Isaiah teaches about receiving strength like that of the eagle—to overcome situations, to rise, to run and to walk, and to continue.

Many times, our focus is only on our problems, but other times, we focus on the wrong thing, like on creatures and not on the Creator, or on a representation of a creator (which is idolatry). But if we lift our eyes to the Lord God Almighty and Wise, to His integral care for His creation and especially His care for us, we will receive strength to carry on with success and victory.

In the first part of Isaiah 40, we see the need for comfort and strength that we receive with complete forgiveness for our sins through Jesus Christ, and the need to prepare our hearts to receive the incorruptible seed of the Word of God.

In the second part of this chapter, the author starts to describe the omnipotent works of the Creator and how He not only has control of everything, He also has a purpose for everything and for everyone. He therefore has the necessary power to help His people in the appropriate way. In addition, the Spirit of the Lord is the best Guide, Counsellor, and Instructor, who can help us understand our ways. We must set our focus only on the Lord, not on any material representation—which is idolatry—nor in any created being or created things—which is also idolatry. This is how we receive strength like the eagles—when we wait on the Lord, to fly, to run and to walk.

Next, there is a call to the people to remember the greatness of the power and the sovereignty of God over His creation. He measured the waters and the heavens, calculated the dust of the earth, weighed the mountains and the hills. These measurements have the purpose of showing beauty and blessing, and He can do the same with His people, making us feel inspired to trust in Him. On one hand, we have the omnipotence of the Lord, and on the other hand the omniscience (He knows everything) of the Spirit of God who guides, counsels, teaches, instructs in righteousness, teaches us in knowledge and shows us the way of intelligence. He is very near, and if we ask Him, He will give us all wisdom and guide us to confront any situation.

We must focus our eyes only and exclusively on Him, the Lord Almighty and Wise, to help us. This means that we should not compare this "only God" with any image of any material—we must not permit idolatry.

Neither should we allow ourselves to see or put our confidence in anyone or anything created, such as a leader, a building, money, our professions, skills, politics, or the nations or systems of philosophies. None of these things free us, and they are in vain.

Finally, besides seeing and remembering the Almighty Wise God, and putting our focus exclusively on Him, we must receive our strength from Him and in the power of His might (Ephesians 6:10). When someone has been born again, he is a new creature with new nature that has potential to overcome any temporary situation. "If anyone is in Christ, he is new creation. The old has passed away; behold, the new has come" (2 Corinthians 5:17, ESV).

The last part of Chapter 40 teaches us that those who wait on the Lord will fly like eagles, they will run and walk with supernatural strength and not be tired.

First, our confidence must not be in ourselves or in our own strength. Young people faint and get weary, "but they who wait for the Lord shall renew their strength; they shall mount up with wings like eagles; they shall run and not be weary; they shall walk and not faint." This means that by depending on the Lord and His strength, one can overcome any temporary difficult situation. We will fly with the strength of an eagle. For that, we need to renew ourselves, leave the past and all that prevents us from only seeing and believing in the Lord, receiving the power He gives. Eagles fly and have very sharp vision from great heights; they renew themselves in order to face the future.

God can give you strength and renew your mind to accept His grace by faith, to depend on Him, to apply the reading and meditation of His Word, and to pray and have fellowship with God. Above all, we must decide to follow Christ (our Teacher), the Holy Spirit (our Instructor), and the Word of God.

We are designed to face situations through His Word, based on the power and wisdom of the Lord, the guidance of the Spirit of the Lord, and to make the decision to acknowledge only Him as Lord. When we wait on the Lord only, He promises to give strength to lift us to a heavenly dimension and to fly with strength to continue our way. When we fly high, we see things better than we do from the ground. The Lord sees the landscape better and counsels us to believe Him and to obey Him. To renew ourselves and fly high, we must leave the past that impedes us from advancing and look toward victory and the high prize that awaits us.

For Meditation and Group Sharing

Isaiah 40:12-31 and the above devotional:

1. From verses 12-14, briefly interpret and name the characteristics of God.

2. How does this exercise help you to focus on these characteristics?

3. In God's sight, the smallness of "the nations" or "the inhabitants" does not mean that He is not interested in them. Explain.

4. Considering who and how God is, what or how is an idol?

5. From verse 23, look for some examples of governments that God put down.

6. Write down verse 23 and speak it out loud.

7. Using verses 28-31, write a response to God for each verse.

8. Where is the focus?

By His Stripes We Have Been Healed

Read Isaiah 53

In a world of difficult circumstances, we need good news of complete and consistent salvation. Someone special announces that He brings news of joy and peace. In His first coming, God the Father presented the Messiah to us as a Lamb, as the suffering Servant of the Lord, who came to make atonement. To fulfill divine justice, He came to take our place, then to take the place of victory against the true enemies of humanity, to take the kingdom and all power.

Isaiah 53 is an explicit picture of the work of Calvary's cross, where holiness, justice, and the wrath of God all meet at the same time—where the eternal love of God restores the relationship with man and his God.

The servant of the Lord

Isaiah 52:7 introduces chapter 53 and mentions someone who brings great news of peace and salvation (in Hebrew "*Yeshua*"). Then in verses 13-14, God the Father says, "Behold my servant" who will be prospered, exalted, and held high, but whose appearance would be disfigured more than any man.

Philippians 2:7-9 (ESV) says that,

> "Christ Jesus emptied himself, taking the form of a servant, made in human form, he humbled himself by becoming obedient to the point of death, even death on a cross. Therefore, God has highly exalted him and bestowed on him the name that is above every name."

At the beginning of chapter 53 we see that this great news must be received by faith and experienced through the power and the strength of God. The Messiah first came to an arid desert and a hostile atmosphere full of outward appearances of holiness, but without faith. His external appearance was nothing attractive, but rather shows His character, full of love and compassion, of holiness, and integrity.

Romans 5:8 says, "But God shows his love toward us in that while we were yet sinners, Christ died for us."

Have you believed and accepted this Christ, and have you appreciated His character internal motives?

Atonement

The suffering of Christ was as "the Lamb of God that takes away the sin of the world" (John 1:29). Atonement, or "*kipur*" in Hebrew, means to erase or take away sin, and (as seen in the Old Testament) is done through an innocent third party as punishment for sin. Sacrifices of innocent lambs without defect were a shadow and figure of the perfect sacrifice of the Messiah. The death of Christ on the cross was a legal act to satisfy divine justice and holiness.

The scripture says, "All we like sheep have gone astray." Sin is universal. Then it says, "We have turned—every one—to his own way." The responsibility is individual. This is why Jesus died. "He was cut off out of the land of the living, stricken for the transgression of my people".

In his body and in His being, Jesus took our sicknesses, and by His stripes we were healed. "We were healed." It is a past action, done completely by Him, and we are the object of the action in the sentence. He is the physician ("*rofe*" in Hebrew), the Lord who heals as part of the atonement. Matthew 8:16-17 (ESV) says,

> "That evening they brought to him many who were oppressed by demons, and he cast out the spirits with a word and healed all who were sick. This was to fulfill what was spoken by the prophet Isaiah: 'He took our illnesses and bore our diseases'."

He died for our physical and spiritual sicknesses. I Peter 2:24, 25 says:

> "He himself bore our sins in his body on the tree, that we might die to sin and live to righteousness. By his wounds you have been healed. For you were straying like sheep but have now returned to the shepherd and overseer of your souls."

The same sacrifice healed our spiritual, emotional, and physical beings; we must only believe, ask Him, and give Him thanks. He redeemed us with the price of his precious blood; he did it voluntarily out of love (John 10:18) to restore us to righteousness and our relationship with God.

In Acts 8:26-39, we see the evangelist Philip use the passage from Isaiah 53 to share the gospel of Jesus to the Ethiopian (who was reading on his journey), and later, he baptized him in water.

Would you like to confess Christ as your Lamb that takes away your sins and heals your sicknesses? Ask Him, believe Him, and give Him thanks.

He died and rose again.

Christ died between two thieves (Matthew 27:38). One of them was saved, acknowledging his guilt and believing in the Holy Lamb of God, in His resurrection, and in His majesty. Christ was with the rich in his death (Matthew 27:57-60). Joseph of Arimathea, a disciple, asked for the body and put it in a new sepulcher fulfilling the prophecy.

Christ died as an Innocent Lamb for us. 2 Corinthians 5:21 (ESV) says, "For our sake he made him to be sin who knew no sin, so that in him we might become the righteousness of God". The cruelty of His death was due to the gravity of sin before the righteousness and holiness of God; His blood has rescued us from sin and our inherited futile manner of living, so we would live by faith in Him (as found in 1 Peter 1:18).

The Messiah-Lamb-Servant of God died for our sin, but He rose and was exalted and now is a High Priest interceding for us at the right hand of the Father.

God loved us so much that He gave His only Son as atonement as an Innocent Lamb that takes away sin. His work on the cross justifies us, He forgives our sins and heals our spiritual, emotional, and physical sicknesses. When we believe and experience the revelation of His power that comes from the cross of Calvary, He gives us peace and joy and an abundant life with purpose, and He puts us in the process of complete restoration of fellowship with God.

The Servant of the Lord, in His first coming, came to make atonement, healing, and restoration; He died and rose to justify us before the Father. Now He is our Intercessor and High Priest at the throne of God, and He will come as King of Kings and Lord of Lords to take the kingdom and power eternally.

For Meditation and Group Sharing

Isaiah 53 and the above devotional:

1. In Isaiah 52:13, what does the author call the Messiah?

2. Write the adjectives in Chapter 53 that describe the Messiah.

3. "The Lord" in this passage refers to God the Father; what did He do, according to the passage?

4. What "peace" or well-being is found as a benefit of all this?

5. According to Isaiah 52:13, what is the final objective of the Messiah?

6. Comment on the word "many" in verses 11 and 12.

7. What is the key word in 53:1 for us now (or rather, since it was fulfilled)?

8. Express your response to the Lord for having imparted this message to Isaiah and for having fulfilled it in His Son.

Life, Health, and Purpose in Coming to the Lord

Read Isaiah 55

Life, strength, and positive results come only from God who is the source of living water and who has made an eternal covenant to all who need, believe, and receive it. The eternal God who loves us calls us to come, listen carefully, seek, and call on Him to receive new life and true nutrition. Due to the suffering Servant-Messiah's work in Isaiah 53, we can obtain the benefits of the eternal covenant made with King David. We must come to the Lord to receive new life and enter the process of transforming our conduct and our way of thinking so we can be useful for the Lord's eternal purposes.

True satisfaction for our soul

The Lord God is speaking personally and calling all who are thirsty without exception. Thirst can be quenched only by drinking water. The imperative "Come" is repeated several times, as are "buy without money", "listen attentively", and "seek", and yet the response to these commands is voluntary. We are invited to come drink water, and to buy wine and milk without money. By faith, everything is free, paid for by Servant of the Lord described in Isaiah 53 and His sacrifice on the cross.

The Lord Jesus said in John 7:37-38 (ESV):

> "On the last day of the feast, the great day, Jesus stood up and cried out, "If anyone thirsts, let him come to me and drink. Whoever believes in me, as the Scripture has said, 'Out of his heart will flow rivers of living water'. Now this he said about the Spirit, who those

> who believed in him were to receive, for as yet the Spirit had not been given, because Jesus was not yet glorified."

Only He can satisfy the deepest needs of our soul. We must evaluate ourselves and ask: Where are our values? What are our priorities in life?

Actions we are to do

Here are several actions or reactions that we are to do in faith.

First, we must come to the Lord and "listen diligently" (attentively) so that our souls will live now and in eternity. The message is of mercy, and of eternal love expressed in compassion, and forgiveness of sins, through the Messiah's eternal covenant in His first coming as Lamb. He gave His body for our sins and sicknesses, and His blood to restore us, to seal His covenant, and to give us joy through His death and resurrection.

After we listen attentively and believe this message, we must "Seek the Lord while he may be found; call upon him while he is near" and forsake our wicked ways and unrighteous thoughts. All have the privilege of seeking Him, but the opportunity is short, so we must take advantage while the Lord and His grace can be found.

Turning to the Lord and abandoning our iniquitous thoughts and wicked ways are part of seeking Him; this is defined as repentance. When we do this, we find the compassion and forgiveness of the Lord.

When we seek the Lord today and take on an attitude of repentance, we need to retrain our way of thinking which brings a change of conduct. Romans 12:1-2 (ESV) says:

> "I appeal to you therefore, brothers, by the mercies of God, to present your bodies as a living sacrifice, holy and acceptable to God, which is your spiritual worship. Do not be conformed to this world, but be transformed by the renewal of your mind, that by testing you may discern what is the will of God, what is good and acceptable and perfect."

We need to consider that His thoughts and His ways are much higher and greater. His wisdom, understanding, and knowledge are perfect and higher and greater than ours; we cannot adapt them to ours. Rather we must adapt our thoughts and ways to His and cultivate an image and likeness of the Son of God through His Word and His Spirit (2 Corinthians 3:18). This brings total confidence and peace.

Retraining the mind is done by the Holy Spirit through the Word of God where we obtain our nutrition, growth, transformation, and victory, similar to a water cycle. As water descends, it fulfills its purpose on the earth, and ascends; so also, the Word of God, without our taking from it or adding to it, fulfills its purpose. This purpose is achieved in restoration, changes, fruits, and results.

The Word of God is a seed in our heart that nourishes us, and it is seed we sow in others.

As the seed of the Word of God works in us, it results in joy and peace that affects both us and others with restorative changes. Instead of drought, barrenness, and uselessness, there will be fruit, usefulness, and beauty, always thanks to His grace and faithfulness.

Lastly, there is an urgent call from the Lord to come before Him with our spiritual needs. First, we drink water without paying and receive the wine and milk of spiritual character which are also free to us; paid for by Jesus, the Lamb of God, on the cross and in His resurrection. To receive this grace, we need faith and repentance, we voluntarily leave our ungodly way of thinking and acting, then continue with the process of resetting our way of thinking through the Word and His Spirit. His thoughts and ways are perfect and, therefore, better than ours. He promises to restore us with his mercy and forgiveness, changing barrenness to a fruitful life, usefulness and spiritual beauty, as we depend on Him and live by faith. All this is for the glory of His name.

For Meditation and Group Sharing

About Isaiah 55

1. Remember occasions when you have spent on something "that does not satisfy".

2. Remember other occasions when you have received something "without money" in which you delighted, perhaps even still.

3. In verse 3, through whom was "the eternal covenant" fulfilled?

4. In verse 6, we read between lines that there is a time when we cannot seek Him. Research this in the Scriptures.

5. The purpose of verses 8 and 9 is not to discourage or distance but to...

6. Explain what the “word that comes from the mouth of God” does, as mentioned in figurative language in verse 10.

7. Verse 13 reminds us of Genesis 3 and the “thorns and thistles”, but here there is a promise: ___ with what basis?

8. We are invited to “Come, listen to me, seek me, return.” Describe how you are doing this in your daily life.

9. Have you enjoyed the results of this passage?

Instructions To Be Heard During Prayer and Fasting

Read Isaiah 58

We need our prayers to God to be answered, so it is important to determine whether we agree with the Word of God. We need to draw near with faith, and faith comes from listening attentively to the Word of God.

Isaiah 58 gives us instructions on how to avoid religious appearances while being another person in daily life. At that time, God's people had a conflict between God's commandment of loving Him integrally and loving one's neighbor, versus ungodly religious rituals in their daily lives. They practiced shameless injustices toward others, but at the same time followed a detailed liturgy. They accused others in order to defend themselves, and had only religious appearances without a true relationship with the Lord or caring for the needy.

When we pray or fast, we need to consider the Word of God that is truth. His word commands us to love the Lord God with all our being and our neighbor as ourselves. We must draw near to God in humility, repentance, sincerity, and faith and evaluate how we relate to our neighbor, according to His Word. Doing this will bring blessings, restoration, and answers to our prayers.

Fasting

Fasting is the total or partial abstinence of food (generally only drinking water) for a day or more with the purpose of drawing near to God in prayer and humility, with urgent petition, to receive answers from God, to break yokes or spiritual blocks, or to take control of our flesh.

On the Day of Atonement or of forgiveness, the people of Israel were commanded to make an annual fast and make a personal and collective evaluation, followed by repentance and changes of attitudes and conduct.

On other occasions of need they were called to fast. For example, in 2 Chronicles 20:3, Jehoshaphat called the people to fast for victory against the enemy; Nehemiah prayed for protection during the construction of the walls of Jerusalem; Daniel fasted with a light diet for revelation of God (Daniel 10:3, 12); Esther fasted for the salvation and protection of her people; Joel (2:12-15) said: "Yet even now, declares the Lord, return to me with all your heart, with fasting, with weeping, and with mourning and rend your hearts and not your garments..."

Problems that need to be dealt with

The first problem that should be declared as transgression and sin is acting as if everything is fine, going through the motions of seeking and knowing the Lord, but living sinfully. Praying for one's own convenience and at the same time, not correcting problems of injustice and disagreements, speaking with iniquity and defending oneself while accusing others, is prideful and done solely for egotistic motives. Fasting to be seen by men, but not in obedience to God, is like the case of the Pharisees in Matthew 6:16-18.

Another problem was keeping the Sabbath only ritually, as an outward law, but without glorifying or resting in the Lord. We can do something good in an incorrect manner; it is not just abstaining from something but also doing what is right in the correct way. Would you like to examine yourself on how your relationship is with God and with your neighbor?

The solution

The solution is found not in avoiding a fast, but in avoiding being superficial, and by evaluating ourselves and confessing our sins to God in repentance. We must decide to have a personal relationship with God in sincerity and humility, study His Word with the Teacher Jesus Christ, and with the instruction of the Holy Spirit, to be taught in the truth that is the source of faith, liberty, and happiness.

We must consider our neighbor (acquaintances, family, coworkers, neighbors) and their various needs, intentionally work to help them, do works of service with generosity and compassion; stop blaming others, forgive, and love our neighbor. Also, change our vocabulary and not speak with iniquity.

Fasting and prayer in this sense involves loosening, releasing, liberating, breaking yokes and spiritual blockage for us and our neighbor.

God's basic commandments are to love Him with sincerity and to love our neighbor in their need.

Regarding the day of rest, we can say that "Christ is our rest" (Hebrews 4:9-10) but it is also necessary to dedicate a day every week to delight in His presence and to rest physically and emotionally, trusting that God is the one who will provide everything.

Results

As a result of attentive listening to the voice of God, repentance and changes in attitudes toward God and conduct toward our neighbors, there will be true changes. Prayer will be answered, there will be light in our paths, vigor and justice in us, and the glory of God will protect us. The Lord's guidance will be on everything, especially in building His kingdom with a solid foundation; there will be restoration, and others will be blessed.

We must pray with sincerity and humility to God and not to men. We must evaluate ourselves and list the things we need to confess to God and abandon them, and of what we need yet to do. Would you like to pray that way right now?

Salvation is by faith in the work of Jesus Christ on the cross. But faith is manifested in works of love in service to others.

Besides ceasing to eat or work, we should do something for others and settle accounts with God.

Colossians 3:23, 24 (ESV) says, "Whatever you do, work heartily, as for the Lord and not for men, knowing that from the Lord you will receive the inheritance as your reward. You are serving the Lord Christ."

For Meditation and Group Sharing

About Isaiah 58

1. In verse 1, who is speaking, and to whom are they speaking? What does He want to be declared, and to whom?

2. What are the three things in verse 2 that should characterize God's people?

3. Explain the difference between external humility and what the Lord asks of us.

4. In verse 7, the Lord rebukes them for their lack of obedience to the "second and great commandment: Love your neighbor as yourself". Explain the connection between Isaiah's words and Jesus' words.

5. What do verses 8-12 say will come from the fast that He demands?

6. Explain the concept of being a "restorer and repairer."

7. There must be prophets like Isaiah to whom God says, like a trumpet: "Declare to my people their sin". This message should not surprise us. Have you ever perceived by the Spirit (not in the flesh!) that God has given you a message of correction for a group?

8. Have you ever noticed God getting someone's attention by speaking through another person?

Biblical Basis For Divine Healing

Follow up to Isaiah 58

The Word of God reveals the will of God regarding everything, especially salvation. It is important to know, believe, and receive the promises of God relating to salvation through Jesus Christ, especially as salvation relates to the healing of the soul and the physical body.

The Word of God instructs us how to increase our faith to receive healing, how to pray, and how to do this based on the promises for healing.

Divine healing was part of the preaching of Jesus Christ and His payment on the cross, and He sent us to lay on healing hands when we preach the gospel. In His church He left the gift of healing (I Corinthians 12:9), and instruction for prayer for the sick anointing with oil and confession for forgiveness of sins (James 5:14-16).

Our physical bodies and our inner beings were created to be healthy. We have an immune system to help us and to protect us against sicknesses. Through medical science and psychology, we can improve our health and prevent and cure sicknesses. God´s desire and prayer should be: "Beloved, I pray that all may go well with you and that you may be in good health, as it goes well with your soul" (3 John 2).

Having a healthy lifestyle—healthy eating, constant exercise, living with inner peace, and loving God and our neighbor—can help prevent many sicknesses.

Salvation:

In the Bible, salvation includes liberation, restoration, and complete wellbeing (*sozo* in Greek). *Yeshua* in Hebrew (in English, "Jesus") means "The Lord saves." The word *shalom* means peace and complete wellbeing.

In Exodus 15:26, we see that the Lord is our Healer—"I am the Lord that heals you"—it is personal. Here we see that we are to listen attentively to instruction to prevent being sick and to have faith in Him who heals.

In Psalm 103:1-3, we see that the Lord forgives all our iniquities and heals all our diseases. We should therefore bless Him, give Him thanks, and praise Him, to receive, by faith, the benefits of salvation.

In Isaiah 53:6, we see that Christ as the Lamb of God went to the cross to take our place and to pay for our sins and our sicknesses.

Faith:

To please God and receive from Him when we come in prayer, we must have faith (Hebrews 11:6). Romans 10:17 says: "Faith comes by hearing and hearing by the word of Christ."

Faith comes from the heart, and we should confess with our mouth. Romans 10:10(ESV): "For with the heart one believes and is justified, and with the mouth one confesses and is saved."

It is important then to know the Word of God regarding salvation, healing, and the way we can receive by faith.

Examples in the gospels:

Mark 5:25-29: A woman with a chronic illness of hemorrhaging first heard about Jesus (faith comes from hearing the message about Christ), then she said to herself: "If I touch even his garments, I will be made well," then she acted and received her health instantly.

Mark 1:41: A leper approached Jesus with an attitude of humility, and worshiping Jesus, said: "If you will, you can make me clean." Jesus with compassion said to him: "I will; be clean." It is interesting to observe the motivation of Jesus to heal, His compassion, and his willingness to heal.

Luke 4:39: Peter's mother-in-law was in bed with a high fever, and they called Jesus to heal her. He rebuked the fever, and she was healed and got up and served Him. Another way of healing is to take authority and order the sickness in the name of Jesus to go away. One of the purposes of being healed is to serve Jesus.

Health and healing are part of God´s salvation through Jesus; it is His will that those who have been saved through faith and by grace, live in health as their souls prosper. And if there is sickness, we should take hold of the faithful promises of God, believe in our hearts, confess with our mouths, and praise Him. Philippians 4:4-7 (ESV) says:

> "Rejoice in the Lord always, and again I say: Rejoice. Let your reasonableness be known to everyone. The Lord is at hand; do not be anxious about anything, but in everything by prayer and supplication with thanksgiving let your requests be made known to God. And the peace of God, which surpasses all understanding, will guard your hearts and your minds in Christ Jesus."

May God bless you with faith in your heart to receive health and healing from the healing God, in the name of Jesus who paid for our sins and our sicknesses on the cross. To Him be glory and honor forever. AMEN

For Meditation and Group Sharing

Isaiah 59 and the above devotional

1. What does the concept "salvation" include in the Bible?

2. In Mark 5:25-29, what were the steps the woman took to receive her healing?

3. What are the purposes that God has in healing us?

4. Besides believing and asking for healing, what should one do to maintain good health?

5. Remember that the body of the believer is "temple of the Holy Spirit" (I Corinthians 6:19 – 20).

6. Copy key verses or phrases about healing:

- Exodus 15:26:

- Psalm 103: 1-3:

- Isaiah 53:5:

7. What does this topic inspire you to do or to express?

Good News For The Afflicted, Broken, Captive and Oppressed

Read Isaiah 61:1, 2

Regardless of what or how many the wounds and chains of the soul may be, it is important to take notice, believe, and receive salvation, liberation, and the restoration that Jesus gives each one of us through His death on the cross. In Isaiah 61:1-2 and Luke 4:18-19, He is the Messiah, the Christ, and speaking in first person.

Anointing consists of consecration and training to carry out a specific function in the mission and call of God. In the Old Testament, anointing was for priests or kings, and for prophets. Jesus was anointed for these same three roles, and in His first coming as a Lamb, His anointing would bring liberation, salvation from sin, and the recuperation and healing from the damages of sin.

It was the year of grace, of jubilee, with forgiveness, liberation, and restoration in His first coming.

In His second coming it will be the day of vengeance of our God. The message of the Messiah in His first coming was directed to the poor, to the brokenhearted, to the oppressed and imprisoned. His message was to heal, liberate, and restore each one who would believe and receive it.

The good news

Beginning in Leviticus 25:10, we see a "year of jubilee" or rest and grace given every 50 years, with rest for the land, forgiveness of debts, freedom of slaves and restoration.

Starting in Luke 4:18, the scripture says that Jesus stood and read the message of jubilee and grace in Isaiah 61:1-2, and then He sat down and said, "Today this Scripture has been fulfilled in your hearing."

Christ came to heal the damage that sin has brought: poverty, wounds in the heart, captivity, and oppression.

Sin impoverishes from all points of view. Christ announces the good news to the afflicted. He has always had a special interest in the poor, especially the poor in spirit. "Blessed are the poor in spirit, for theirs is the kingdom of heaven" (Matthew 5:3). In Luke 18:9-14, we see the Pharisee and the publican praying, but only the latter is justified before God because of his humility and his dependence on God´s mercy.

Sin breaks hearts, but Christ comes with oil and the wine of the Holy Spirit to heal and to bind up the broken in their traumas and wounds from the past.

Sin imprisons, takes captive and oppresses, but Christ gives freedom to the captive and opens the doors of the prison for prisoners. Acts 10:38 says, "God anointed Jesus of Nazareth with the Holy Spirit and with power. He went about doing good and healing all who were oppressed by the devil, for God was with him."

Sin is a crime that must be judged and punished, and Christ paid and suffered that punishment on the cross. Colossians 2:14 says: "...Canceling the record of debt that stood against us with its legal demands. This he set aside, nailing it to the cross."

The good Samaritan (Luke 25:30-37)

In the parable of the good Samaritan, the man who was assaulted, wounded, and left half dead, was not helped by religious people or by religion. He was helped by one who had compassion and had the elements of wine and oil to cure (these are types of the Holy Spirit), and to take him to a safe place. In this place, which was an inn, they followed-up with restoration.

With the same price that Jesus, our Good Samaritan, paid on the cross to forgive our sins, He also restores us with love and the power of the Holy Spirit. As we give ourselves to His Word and His specific work in us, we prepare for His second coming as King. Would you like to come to Jesus in humility, acknowledging Him as the anointed one to forgive you, free you and restore you?

The Scripture of Isaiah 61:1-2 that Jesus read in Luke 4:18, is fulfilled in us when we hear it, believe it, and receive it. It is fulfilled when we come to the cross of Christ just as we are, confessing Him as Lord and Savior, with humility and trusting in His compassion and asking Him to heal our wounds and to set us free.

Afterwards, we must enter the process of restoration through His Word and His Holy Spirit.

"Come to me, all you that are weary and heavy laden, and I will give you rest. Take my yoke upon you and learn of me, for I am meek and lowly of heart, and you will find rest for your souls. My yoke is easy, and my burden is light" (Matthew 11:29 – 30).

For Meditation and Group Sharing

Isaiah 61:1-2 and the above devotional:

1. According to verse 1, what has the Lord done to the one speaking?

2. What kinds of people need what He has?

3. Which other group is mentioned in what Jesus read in Luke?

4. What did Jesus mean when He said: Today this Scripture is fulfilled that you have heard?

5. Research and describe the definitions or concepts of:
   - affliction:

   - brokenness:

   - captive:

   - prisoner:

6. Research and define the biblical concepts of:
   - salvation:

   - deliverance:

   - restoration:

7. According to the above devotional, what does sin do in a person or a group?

8. What did Jesus do about sin? Explain thoroughly, with Scriptural basis.

9. Describe a personal experience of being or feeling "afflicted, broken, captive or prisoner".

10. What has happened so that you are not that way now?

Comfort That Jesus Brings as Messiah and Its Results

Read Isaiah 61:2b – 11

In his first coming as Servant, Christ bought our salvation on the cross, suffering and paying the punishment for our peace. This peace includes healing, liberation, revelation, consolation, strength, happiness, joy, jubilee, and a new life that He gives us in His grace and love.

The people of Israel returned from exile in Babylonia with the help of King Cyrus of Persia, and the Lord comforted them and assigned to them the reconstruction of Jerusalem and the work of agriculture. But during this process, there were difficulties to conquer with determination and faith in the promises of restoration of the Lord.

Jesus, the Messiah, comforts us, dresses us with joy and happiness, transfers us to His kingdom, forgives our sins, and gives us hope, position, and identity in His family. He assigns functions of intercession, worship, reconstruction, and planting, all which bring change inside us and impact our surroundings.

The comfort of Christ

Christ, the Anointed, came the first time to give good news to those who acknowledge their spiritual need, to those that weep, to those that are hungry and thirsty for righteousness, who believe and receive, because for them He bought salvation on the cross.

There is a lifting of the burdens of the one who comes to Christ. When we believe, repent, and change our way of thinking, He gives us identity as children, with a crown instead of ashes, a garment of praise and joy instead of a faint spirit. This is what Christ did for us on the cross and as a result, the Holy Spirit comes to do follow up, filling us with His presence, especially during our praise, strengthening us, guiding us, and teaching us. All this is by grace and faith, so that only God is glorified.

Rebuilding

We first receive the good news of healing, liberation, and spiritual vision or revelation by the Holy Spirit of our position and function. We acquire that vision as we study the Word of God and apply it and have fellowship with God.

We must rebuild our spiritual, moral, and physical lives and those of others, with faith and persistence, just as the Israelites did when they returned from exile. Basing our attitudes on the promises of God, despite our difficulties, we will be like oak trees of righteousness, strong and useful. We restore fellowship with God, building our lives, our families, and our society based on the values of the kingdom of heaven.

The covenant

The Lord is a God of covenants since the beginning of humanity. According to Jeremiah 31:31, the Lord establishes a new covenant, and according to Jeremiah 32:40, "I will make with them an everlasting covenant that I will not turn from doing good to them, and I will put the fear of me in their hearts, that they may not turn from me."

2 Corinthians 3:6 says, "Who has made us sufficient to be ministers of a new covenant, not of the letter but of the Spirit. For the letter kills, but the Spirit gives life."

Referring to the covenant that Jesus Christ made when He died on the cross, with His blood He made an eternal covenant. Mark 14:24 says, "And He said: This is my blood of the new covenant, that is poured out for many."

With the new covenant sealed with the blood of Christ, we have forgiveness of sins and free entrance to the presence of God.

Fruit

The results of believing and applying the Word of God are evident in our society and communities. We see it in the book of Acts, in the Reformation of the sixteenth century in Europe, and in the revivals of the Christian Church throughout history. Its effects will be recognized among the nations, statistically in the indicators of human development, when changes are substantial, because a new generation can be taught to think and to act with ethics and with changes.

The Word of God is a seed in the heart and its fruit grows in individuals, families, and social groups who shine as lights and are salt in a society that needs to come out of darkness and corruption.

Justification is the legal act in which God declares us righteous by faith in Christ Jesus, to live a righteous life and have works of righteousness as a garment. Ephesians 4:24 says, "And that you put on the new man, which, in the likeness of God, has been created in righteousness and holiness in the truth," to prepare for the coming of the Lord Jesus Christ and to be in the wedding feast of the Lamb.

Revelation 19:7-8 says: "Let us rejoice and exult and give Him the glory, for the marriage of the Lamb has come, and his Bride has made herself ready; it was granted her to clothe herself with fine linen, bright and pure."

All this fulfills God's plans for His creation and in the future world for the praise of His Name.

To put on joy and happiness, we must accept the Good News of salvation, healing, and liberation through the cross of Calvary, as well as accepting the revelation of the Holy Spirit, in order to see the reality of the Word of God. We must believe in Him and praise His Name, seeking Him in prayer, believing and receiving by faith the grace of the Lord Jesus Christ, be willing to bear fruit, interceding, and preparing ourselves for the second coming of the Lord and the wedding feast of the Lamb of God.

For Meditation and Group Sharing

Isaiah 61:2b-11 and the above devotional

1. How do we know that this passage refers to the One who would come, Jesus?

2. Summarize in a few words what He was going to do.

3. In verse 4, who then "will rebuild?"

4. Verse 8 gives the reason behind all that the Lord does. Please explain.

5. According to verse 9, which benefits of the works of the Lord extend to the "descendants"?

6. Make a drawing that represents what verses 3 and 10 say.

7. Express your response to this chapter (and Luke 4: 18).

8. The same Holy Spirit that filled and came over Jesus, fills and comes over those who believe, follow and love Him. So, what could or should happen as a result?

Bibliography

Beers, V. Gilbert. Un Viaje a traves de la Biblia (Journey through the Bible). Tyndale House Publishers, Inc. Carol stream, Illinois. 2010

Biblia de Estudio de la Biblia de las Américas (Study Bible of the Americas). B&H español. Nashville Tennessee. 2000

Compendio Manual de la Biblia (Halley's Bible Handbook) por Henry H. Halley. Editorial Moody 1924.

Estudios de Hebreo bíblico en "e-teacher" (español-hebreo) (Biblical Hebrew Studies). Niveles A,B,C,D,E. The Hebrew University of Jerusalem, Israel. 2016

Guzic, David (ES) commentaries. E-Sword-the Sword of the LORD with an electronic edge. Date unknown.

La Biblia de las Américas (The Bible of the Americas). Editor R.C. Sproul – 2020

La Biblia de la Reforma, Biblia de estudio Reina Valera Contemporánea. Editorial Concordia (The Bible of the Reformation, Reina Valera Contemporary Study Bible). Saint Louis MO, U.SA. 2014

Morrissey, Baroness Helena (for the expression on page 76: "Think big, start small, start now".)

About The Author

I was born into a Christian family in the western highlands in Guatemala, the third of three children. When I was a year old, after a rainstorm that destroyed my father's wheat mill, my family moved to the urban area of Guatemala. I lived my first thirteen years in a house with a dirt floor, with no electricity or running water.

My dad was the intermediary for the sale of the land for the future campus of the government-owned University of San Carlos of Guatemala, in the city of Quetzaltenango. Years later, he worked in this university as janitor and watchman.

Throughout my childhood and youth, my family walked over two miles to church, day or night. From first through twelfth grade, I walked about that same distance every day to get to public school.

I studied medicine and graduated from the same university where my father worked, and then for four years, I worked for World Vision International in rural communities, mostly to improve the growth and development of children and sometimes to provide medical care to mothers. For 32 years, I was a professor of Biostatistics in the Health Sciences Department in the San Carlos University. I also obtained master's degrees in University Education and in Public Health Administration and served on a thesis committee for medical school graduates.

In Guatemala, I was an usher in church, a discipleship leader, and pastoral helper. Also, I opened a mobile evangelistic clinic in many rural areas in Guatemala.

In 2013, I wrote a book: "Visión y Desarrollo de la Iglesia Evangélica en Quetzaltenango, Guatemala" (The Vision and Development of the Evangelical Church in Quetzaltenango, Guatemala), which was used in several Bible institutes.

I am married and have three children, all university graduates, who have given us nine grandchildren. My wife and I moved to the United States just before the Covid-19 pandemic, and we all now live in the Seattle area.

In August of 2020, I started the "Edificación Integral" YouTube channel, where I have presented weekly short videos with reflections in Spanish. My motivation in creating this channel was to comfort and share hope from the Scriptures, initially amid the COVID-19 pandemic.

This book is the compilation and translation of these reflections.

Connect with Saul: **Facebook**: Saul Lopez
Instagram: Saulofish

www.ingramcontent.com/pod-product-compliance
Ingram Content Group UK Ltd.
Pitfield, Milton Keynes, MK11 3LW, UK
UKHW062258290726
14090UKWH00017B/766

9 798992 761009